Lectionary Stories for Preaching and Teaching

Series II, Cycle C

Peter Andrew Smith

CSS Publishing Company, Inc.
Lima, Ohio

LECTIONARY STORIES FOR PREACHING AND TEACHING
SERIES II, CYCLE C

FIRST EDITION
Copyright © 2015
by CSS Publishing Co., Inc.

Published by CSS Publishing Company, Inc., Lima, Ohio 45807. All rights reserved. No part of this publication may be reproduced in any manner whatsoever without the prior permission of the publisher, except in the case of brief quotations embodied in critical articles and reviews. Inquiries should be addressed to: CSS Publishing Company, Inc., Permissions Department, 5450 N. Dixie Highway, Lima, Ohio 45807.

For more information about CSS Publishing Company resources, visit our website at www.csspub.com, email us at csr@csspub.com, or call (800) 241-4056.

e-book:
ISBN-13: 978-0-7880-2837-3
ISBN-10: 0-7880-2837-5

ISBN-13: 978-0-7880-2836-6
ISBN-10: 0-7880-2836-7

PRINTED IN USA

*To Meredith whose love and support
has allowed me to go further
than I ever dreamt possible
and to Hope whose arrival
during this book
was both a joy and a surprise.
I love you both.*

Book Reviews

Readers will recognize themselves in the characters of these stories and their everyday circumstances. They live in the light of God's grace and love, finding their way through life's challenges with prayer and the gentle encouragement of friends, family, and neighbors.

These are stories that all ages will appreciate: understandable to children but with depth and wisdom for older generations as well. Smith presents the Christian life in a hope-filled and down-to-earth way.

This book is a great treasure, following a full cycle of the lectionary, beginning in Advent and advancing through the liturgical year. Preachers and readers of the lectionary will delight in how closely the themes of these stories relate to the biblical texts we love so well.

Best of all, Smith's writing reminds us of the goodness of following Jesus each day with trusting faith, and the difference this makes in our lives and the lives of those around us.

Robert C. Fennell
Associate Professor of Historical and Systematic Theology
Atlantic School of Theology, Halifax, Nova Scotia
rfennell@astheology.ns.ca

We humans are a curious and storytelling people. Stories help us communicate information and teach us something about ourselves and our world. Stories also help explain the unexplainable. This is why they hold such an important place in the life and work of our faith communities. Stories invite us into a deeper reflection of the text being preached on each Sunday and they help us think about how we can respond to the call of these readings.

In our day to day work lives, however, it becomes increasingly difficult to find time to write stories that inform, educate and inspire listeners. This is why Peter Smith's book, entitled Lectionary Stories for Preaching and Teaching is so important. Peter offers us a series of stories grounded in the weekly lectionary readings that offer structure to our church's worship calendar. These stories invite us into the text and they also help us introduce and illustrate the themes and ideas contained within each and every one. These stories are a real blessing and gift to preachers and service leaders everywhere and I hope that each and every one has a chance to read and use *Lectionary Stories for Preaching and Teaching*.

Michael K. Jones
Empty Houses: A Pastoral Approach to Congregational Closures and Dead Reckoning: The Six Phases of a Funeral (upcoming)

Foreword

I think faith is something best explained through story. When we use a story to share what we believe we do not merely tell others our faith, we invite them to experience that truth for themselves. Whether the great narratives of the Bible, the parables of Jesus, or the lives of the saints, stories have long been the way we express the spiritual truths and concepts which can not be captured by other means. Stories open the world to us in a way greater than the actual words which form them. They help us to encounter truth, view the world differently, and confront life.

A narrative allows us experience emotions and perspectives in order to grow deeper in understanding and wisdom. We can be a traveler seeing a wounded stranger by the side of the road, a woman searching for a lost coin, or a king caught in his misdeeds by a prophet. We can be tested and challenged by the best behaviours and the worst actions as we come face to face with our hidden thoughts and hear God whispering from the narrative. For stories told in faith and listened to in faith allow us to catch a glimpse of who God is and what God asks from us.

Stories also stay with us. We hear them and then carry them in our heads and our hearts, reliving the words and re-experiencing the events. Within each story there are different perspectives and views for us to consider which offer both comfort and discomfort. For we can also be the wounded man longing to be saved by those passing by, the coin waiting to be found, and the prophet denouncing the king. The power of the narrative is that it keeps speaking to us long after we have initially heard and thought about the words.

This book contains 66 stories intended to help preachers and those studying the Bible to explore deeper the words of the gospel lesson from the lectionary cycle. Each story seeks to express a truth from within the text and help us gain new insight. Each one is written with the intention of fostering spiritual growth and wisdom in our lives.

The stories in this book were written after prayerful consideration of the texts referenced. Some flowed easily from start to finish and others had a more difficult path from draft to final form. I appreciate the support and help of many people along the way.

Thanks to my wife Meredith who helped me clarify and refine some of the theological concepts. Thanks to Anne Louise, John, and John who offered suggestions and feedback during our writers group. Thanks to David who offered me the opportunity to write these stories and to Missy and Sue at CSS for their support and encouragement.

My hope and prayer is that these stories will help you, challenge you, and inspire you in your faith.

Soli Deo Gloria,

Peter,
July 2015

Table of Contents

Advent 1, *Luke 21:25-36*	11
When Tomorrow Comes	
Advent 2, *Luke 3:1-6*	14
Ready to Welcome	
Advent 3, *Luke 3:7-18*	17
The Sound of Good News	
Advent 4, *Luke 1:39-45 (46-55)*	20
God's Grace Makes Anything Possible	
Christmas Eve / Day, *Luke 2:1-14 (15-20)*	23
Welcoming God's Love	
Christmas 1, *Luke 2:41-52*	27
The Days after Christmas	
Christmas 2, *John 1:(1-9) 10-18*	30
Grace Filled	
New Year's Day, *Matthew 25:31-46*	33
Whatever You Do	
Epiphany of Our Lord, *Matthew 2:1-12*	36
Finding the Light	
Baptism of Our Lord, *Luke 3:15-17, 21-22*	39
Expectations	
Epiphany 2, *John 2:1-11*	42
What Comes Next?	
Epiphany 3, *Luke 4:14-21*	45
Seeing the Kingdom	
Epiphany 4, *Luke 4:21-30*	48
Unwelcome Words	
Epiphany 5, *Luke 5:1-11*	51
Unexpected Blessings	
Epiphany 6, *Luke 6:17-26*	54
Acceptable to God	
Epiphany 7, *Luke 6:27-38*	57
Like the Most High	
Epiphany 8, *Luke 6:39-49*	60
A Solid Foundation	
Transfiguration of Our Lord, *Luke 9:28-36 (37-43)*	63
The Experience of a Lifetime	

Ash Wednesday, *Matthew 6:1-6, 16-21* — 67
   What Jesus Asks
Lent 1, *Luke 4:1-13* — 70
   Answering Temptation
Lent 2, *Luke 13:31-35* — 73
   What You Believe
Lent 3, *Luke 13:1-9* — 77
   Following the Way
Lent 4, *Luke 15:1-3, 11b-32* — 80
   Answering with Grace
Lent 5, *John 12:1-8* — 83
   Worship and Service
Passion / Palm Sunday, *Luke 19:28-40* — 86
   Seeds of Faith
Maundy Thursday, *John 13:1-17, 31b-35* — 89
   Priorities in Life
Good Friday, *John 18:1—19:42* — 93
   Hearing the Good News
Easter Sunday, *John 20:1-18* — 96
   New Beginnings
Easter 2, *John 20:19-31* — 99
   Answering Doubt
Easter 3, *John 21:1-19* — 102
   Faithful Bounty
Easter 4, *John 10:22-30* — 105
   Knowing His Voice
Easter 5, *John 13:31-35* — 108
   As I Have Loved You
Easter 6, *John 14:23-28* — 111
   Finding Peace
Ascension of Our Lord, *Luke 24:44-53* — 114
   Witness to These Things
Easter 7, *John 17:20-26* — 117
   Together as One
Pentecost Day, *John 14:8-17 (25-27)* — 120
   Never Alone
Trinity Sunday, *John 16:12-15* — 123
   Always Together

Proper 4/ Pentecost 2 / Ordinary Time 9, *Luke 7:1-10*   126
  Finding Faith
Proper 5 / Pentecost 3 / Ordinary Time 10, *Luke 7:11-17*   129
  Resurrection Hope
Proper 6 / Pentecost 4 / Ordinary Time 11, *Luke 7:36—8:3*   132
  Witness of the Sinful
Proper 7 / Pentecost 5 / Ordinary Time 12, *Luke 8:26-39*   135
  A New Life
Proper 8 / Pentecost 6 / Ordinary Time 13, *Luke 9:51-62*   138
  Being Ready
Proper 9 / Pentecost 7 / Ordinary Time 14,
    Luke 10:1-11, 16-20   141
  Grounded in Faith
Proper 10 / Pentecost 8 / Ordinary Time 15, *Luke 10:25-37*   144
  Being a Neighbor
Proper 11 / Pentecost 9 / Ordinary Time 16, *Luke 10:38-42*   147
  Two Paths
Proper 12 / Pentecost 10 / Ordinary Time 17, *Luke 11:1-13*   150
  Learning to Pray
Proper 13 / Pentecost 11 / Ordinary Time 18, *Luke 12:13-21*   153
  Being Rich
Proper 14 / Pentecost 12 / Ordinary Time 19, *Luke 12:32-40*   156
  Sharing the Wealth
Proper 15 / Pentecost 13 / Ordinary Time 20, *Luke 12:49-56*   159
  The Difficult Way
Proper 16 / Pentecost 14 / Ordinary Time 21, *Luke 13:10-17*   162
  The Rule of Love
Proper 17 / Pentecost 15 / Ordinary Time 22, *Luke 14:1, 7-14*   166
  Learning in Humility
Proper 18 / Pentecost 16 / Ordinary Time 23, *Luke 14:25-33*   169
  First Things First
Proper 19 / Pentecost 17 / Ordinary Time 24, *Luke 15:1-10*   172
  Divine Persistence
Proper 20 / Pentecost 18 / Ordinary Time 25, *Luke 16:1-13*   175
  Who Do You Serve?
Proper 21 / Pentecost 19 / Ordinary Time 26, *Luke 16:19-31*   178
  No Greater Witness

Proper 22 / Pentecost 20 / Ordinary Time 27, *Luke 17:5-10* 181
   Faithful Servants
Proper 23 / Pentecost 21 / Ordinary Time 28, *Luke 17:11-19* 184
   Thankful Harvest
Proper 24 / Pentecost 22 / Ordinary Time 29, *Luke 18:1-8* 187
   Powerful Persistence
Proper 25 / Pentecost 23 / Ordinary Time 30, *Luke 18:9-14* 190
   The Humble Soul
Proper 26 / Pentecost 24 / Ordinary Time 31, *Luke 19:1-10* 193
   Who Is Worthy?
Proper 27 / Pentecost 25 / Ordinary Time 32, *Luke 20:27-38* 196
   Honoring the Word
Proper 28 / Pentecost 26 / Ordinary Time 33, *Luke 21:5-19* 199
   Considering Our Priorities
Christ the King (Proper 29) / Pentecost 27 /
   Ordinary Time 34, *Luke 23:33-43* 202
   Heavenly Reception
Reformation Day, *John 8:31-36* 205
   Being Set Free
All Saints Day, *Luke 6:20-31* 208
   Blessed Are You
Thanksgiving Day, *John 6:25-35* 211
   Hungering and Thirsting for More

Advent 1
Luke 21:25-36

When Tomorrow Comes

Jane slammed her hands against the steering wheel as the engine died. She didn't have time for this. She was going to be late for her appointment and she wouldn't be able to get groceries before school finished. That meant she would have to deal with the twins whining about being hungry and wanting to go home while trying to shop. She glanced at her watch. The store would be crowded and that would make them late for supper. There was no way she was going to arrive before her shift started at the mall.

She turned the key but the engine refused to start. A knot formed in her stomach. Mr. Lewis would dock her pay for being late. He might even decide to let her go. As much as she hated working retail she needed that job and if she got fired she didn't know what she would do. She smelled gas and buried her face in her hands. There was no way she was going to be able to afford repairs to the car on top of all the other bills.

A knock on the window made her jump in her seat. Mr. Simons, the elderly man who lived upstairs in their apartment building, gestured to her and she rolled down her window.

"Everything okay?"

"Fine." Jane forced herself to smile. "My car does this sometimes."

"Do you want me to call for a tow truck?" He pulled out his cell phone.

"No."

"Is there someone you can call then?" He handed her the phone through the open window.

"There is no one I can call." Jane handed the phone back to him. She tried the key again with no success. "My car has to start."

"It might be that you just flooded it," Mr. Simons said.

"Is that serious?"

"It means that you can't start the car right now."

She turned the key again. "But I need to get going."

"If you keep trying you might end up ruining the battery."

"Is that serious?"

"It will mean you have to replace it," he said.

"I can't afford that." She wiped a tear from her cheek.

"Can I give you a lift?" he asked.

"I need my car because I have to get to an appointment, pick up food, and get the twins home and fed before my sister comes over. I can't be late for work again."

Mr. Simons reached into his pocket and pulled out a key. "I don't need my truck this afternoon. Run your errands and get the girls. Your car will probably start if you let it sit for a couple of hours."

Jane got out of her car. "Are you sure?"

"I wouldn't be offering it if I wasn't sure."

"But you don't really know me," she said. "We've never spoken more than a hello before today."

"I saw you at church at Thanksgiving and I know you have two little girls and live in the apartment below me." He handed her the key. "I don't need to know anything more."

"I hope they aren't too noisy."

"They are busy and active but honestly since I am by myself now I don't mind hearing the noise." He smiled. "Go run your errands."

"I don't know how I can repay you."

"The good book says that neighbors should help neighbors," he said. "You don't owe me anything."

"Really? There is nothing I can do to return the favor?"

"Well, I see you running here and there with your girls and I know that you're busy." He paused. "If you would, I wish you would take a bit of advice from an old man."

"What's that?"

"Don't let your worries and cares get a hold of you so much," he said. "You can get trapped when you lose sight of what's important in life and end up missing the good things God has planned for you."

"Sometimes it seems like life is working against me." She sighed. "Things are so busy when I work nights that it's hard to get to church on Sunday morning."

"That's the way life can be. Always remember, though, the eternal truths God has promised and that will keep you focused."

"Even if we don't always get to church, I try to teach the girls to be good people."

"Just don't forget to teach them to be God's people too," he said. "Now get yourself to your errands before you're late."

When Jane got into the truck, she noticed the Bible and the program from the church sitting on the front seat. She thought about Mr. Simon's advice on the drive to her appointment and realized that she wanted the twins to know more about God than she was able to teach them. As she pulled into the parking lot of the medical clinic, she decided that no matter what happened that week they would all be going to church on Sunday.

Advent 2
Luke 3:1-6

Ready to Welcome

"Todd, it's time to get up!"

Todd rolled over and groaned. "Dad, it's early. Can't I sleep a little more?"

"No, you can't." His father appeared in the doorway. "It snowed last night so we have to get things ready at the church."

Todd grumbled as he got dressed and ate some cereal. His father was waiting at the door and handed him a snow shovel as soon as his boots were tied. They trudged side by side down the street.

"Why do we need to clear the snow, Dad?"

"We need to prepare the way so that people can get to worship." His father pointed toward the church. "Can you get the ramp while I start on the stairs?"

Todd began shovelling the wet, heavy snow. It was hard work and his muscles began to ache. His father reappeared with a bucket of salt.

"Don't forget this when you are finished."

"I'm shoveling it." Todd looked at the area he had already cleared. "That should be enough."

"Well, we don't want anyone to slip getting into church, do we?" his father asked.

Todd thought of Mrs. Jones and Mr. Tanaka and some of the other people who walked up the ramp. Most of them needed canes or walkers and were unsteady on their feet. "I doubt they will come out to church on a day like today."

"But what if they do? Would you want them to make the effort to get here and discover that they can't come into the worship service?"

"Todd sighed. "I guess not."

"That's the spirit, Son." His father patted him on the back. "Make sure that the way is as clear as you can make it."

"My arms are getting tired," Todd said. "I don't know how much more I can do."

"You've got the worst of it done. I'm going to clear the choir door." His father stopped and looked at him. " Don't forget that this is a very important job."

Todd rolled his eyes.

"Seriously, son. We're making sure that people can come to God." His father tilted his head. "I guess you can say we're like John the Baptist."

"Right, Dad." Todd thought of the Vacation Bible School when Pastor Cho told them all about John the Baptist and the verse from Isaiah about him preparing the way. "Just don't try making me eat locusts."

His father laughed heartily and disappeared around the building. Todd put his shovel on the ramp and gave a half-hearted push. His father was always enthusiastic about doing things in the morning while all Todd wanted to do was go back to bed.

"I told you they would be clearing the snow, George."

Todd turned to see Mrs. Shepherd pushing her son George in his wheelchair. George waved at him and gave a big smile. Todd waved back.

"George was sure that there was no way he could get into church today but I told him that when it stormed that Todd and his father would be here to make sure that the ramp and doors were cleared." Mrs. Shepherd looked at the remaining snow. "Are you going to be much longer, Todd?"

15

Todd shoveled quickly and finished the top of the ramp. He stepped back and looked at his handiwork. "Just be careful. I haven't put the salt down on it."

"Okay dear." Mrs. Shepherd pushed George up the ramp. "You're such a thoughtful young man."

Todd stepped to one side as he put the shovel down and picked up the salt bucket. George waved again as he passed by.

Todd started putting salt on the ramp as people began to arrive for church. They all said hello and commented on what a good job he was doing. Todd felt a warm glow as he finished his work.

His father reappeared. "I see Mrs. Shepherd and George came despite the snow. Ready to go in?"

Todd looked over at the ramp. "Is service starting now?"

"No, there are still a few minutes before things begin. I thought your arms were tired."

"They are," Todd said "But I want to make sure the sidewalk leading up to the ramp has salt on it so that so it won't be slippery for any people rushing at the last minute."

"Sounds good to me." His father grabbed another salt bucket and started helping. Together, father and son worked to make sure that the way was not merely clear for the people wanting to come to God but also that it was inviting and welcoming.

Advent 3
Luke 3:7-18

The Sound of Good News

"What do you mean I would be in the junior category?" Johnny asked.

Roger motioned his assistant to hand out football camp brochures to the teens gathered around the booth. He stepped to one side with Johnny.

"That's what your evaluation says."

Johnny hook his head. "You must be looking at the wrong name."

"Johnny Von Holden from Spring Street here in town?" Roger ran his finger down the list on his clipboard.

"Yes, that's me."

"There's no mistake. Junior category to start. That's two practices a day plus one classroom. Scrimmages at the end of the week."

"Practices? You mean I wouldn't even get to play?"

"If you want to get better you have to practice."

"I'm a great player." Johnny frowned. "You guys must be making a mistake."

"Johnny, I was at your last game and did the evaluation myself. You know the basics and are a decent sprinter." Roger thumbed through his clipboard until he found the page he wanted. "However you get winded after a couple of plays and tend to throw the ball wildly at times."

"We won the game!"

"The other team wasn't that good." Roger closed his clipboard. "If you register for this camp you would be put in the junior category. You need work on the fundamentals."

"I threw two touchdowns," Johnny said.

"They were short throws and on one of them you were lucky it didn't get intercepted."

"Are you serious?" Johnny's face grew warm. "You're telling me I'm no good as a football player and I need lots of practice?"

"I'm telling you the truth." Roger looked him in the eye. "You have the potential for being a great ball player but you need to master some skills before you get there."

Johnny thrust the brochure into his pocket and stormed off. He worked his way along the other booths in the conference center promoting sports camps. He saw a couple of kids carrying footballs with a logo on them and asked where they got them. They all pointed him toward a booth near the back. The man behind the table was wearing a licensed football jersey and the sign behind him showed professional players. The man flashed a toothy smile.

"So you looking for a football camp?"

"Yeah, I am," Johnny said. "What's your camp like?"

"Best camp there is if I do say so myself. We have air conditioning in the dorms and an ice cream bar in the cafeteria." The man thrust out his hand. "I'm Jock. What's your name?"

"Johnny Van Holden. I play quarterback for our school."

"I bet you're good."

Johnny stood a little taller. "I'm a great player."

Jock clapped him on the shoulder. "Awesome. We have a jersey for everyone who attends and sometimes we get pros who come in to visit."

"Who?"

Jock leaned forward. "I can't say because the press would be all over it but believe me they are famous."

"Sweet." Johnny looked at the familiar faces of the players on the banner behind Jock. "What class would I be in?"

18

Jock looked him up and down. "I think you would probably be in the advanced class since you already play."

"Nice."

"All I would need is your address and a down payment from your parents and we could get you signed up." Jock handed him a form.

"You don't need to evaluate me?"

"Why would I need to do that? You told me you're a great player and that's good enough for me." Jock looked around and then handed him a football from under the table. "I don't say this to everyone, but I know you're the type of up-and-comer we want in our advanced class. If you sign up you get one of these to take home."

Johnny noticed the ball had the same logo on it as the ones he had seen earlier. "Everyone going to your camp get a ball like this?"

Jock shook his head. "Only the advanced class deserves these beauties."

"I'll talk to my parents and let you know." Johnny handed the ball back.

Jock turned to greet another teen. Johnny recognized him as a substitute who rarely got to play. He watched as Jock pulled out a football for the advanced class and handed it to him. Johnny went to find his mother.

"So did you find a camp to go to this year?" she asked.

"I think I did, Mom." Johnny paused. "Can it be good news when someone tells you something you don't want to hear?"

"Yes, good news can sometimes be hard to take," his mother said. "Especially when it's the truth and is going to make you a better person."

"Then I would like you to come with me and meet Roger." Johnny turned himself around. "I want to go to the camp he is running."

19

Advent 4
Luke 1:39-45 (46-55)

God's Grace Makes Anything Possible

She cradled her newly born child and said a prayer of thanks to God that she was so richly blessed. The pregnancy had been difficult and the delivery long but now she held her son in her arms. The newborn snuggled in her embrace and she drew him close and whispered, "God's grace can make anything possible."

She took him home and worked a shift in the corner store while he slept and spent as much time as she could with him. She was there when he rolled over and rejoiced when he stood without any help. She wept when he took his first steps. She wrapped him in her arms and said, "God's grace can make anything possible."

She started a second job when he went to school in order to provide him with everything he needed. She came to every play and concert he was in and made sure she was there to take him to every doctor visit when he was sick. She took him to church on Sunday and taught him to pray at mealtime and bedtime. She read him a story from the Bible each night and told him of Jesus' unending love. Each night before he fell asleep she gently kissed his forehead and said, "God's grace can make anything possible."

She was proud when he grew and started to do things on his own. She let him choose his own friends and find his own way in the world. However, she insisted that each meal time they ate together and he continued to go to church with her even when he claimed he was tired or that it was boring.

At the end of each day, she looked in on him and before she closed the door whispered, "God's grace can make anything possible."

The day he graduated high school was one of the happiest days of her life. She attended every event and despite his objections even chaperoned the prom. From a distance she watched her boy who was now growing into a man talk with his friends and dance with a girl that he secretly liked. When he received his diploma tears ran down her face and after the ceremony she held him close and said "God's grace can make anything possible." He asked her why she always said that and she replied, "Because those words are true."

She didn't say anything when he flunked out of college and half-heartedly worked a series of dead end jobs. He ignored her advice and example, and went through a series of meaningless relationships that resulted in a couple of unwanted children. Someone promised him some easy money if he did a favor for them and he found himself alone and in prison. She prayed for him as he sat in the cell and wrote to her about how his life had taken such a wrong turn. She knew he was terrified as he went before the judge and the sentence was announced. She saw in his face that he didn't know how he was possibly going to get through being in prison for that long. He couldn't look at her as they led him away but she knew he heard her say, "God's grace can make anything possible."

Her words followed him on the bus as he was taken away in chains. He didn't believe they were true but dared to hope that his life was supposed to be more than the mess he had made of it. That first night locked away he prayed and asked God to help him. He stayed away from the gangs and the drugs behind bars. He went to every service that was held in the chapel. He made friends with other inmates trying to stay clean and together they supported each other through the difficult days.

The parole board offered him early release because of his conduct inside and he was set free. The chaplain from the prison asked him to help work in a ministry for ex-cons and addicts who were trying to get their lives together after they got out. He worked hard at it. He made time for the children he had fathered who had grown into boys while he was in prison and helped support them. He tried to make amends.

His mother came to the first service he preached at when he told his story of being a convict and how God had helped turn his life around. She came up to him with tears in her eyes. "I am so proud of you."

"Mom," he replied. "I'm an ex-con and a recovering addict. I have had children out of wedlock and struggle to make it through each day on the outside. How can you say you are proud of me?"

She opened her arms to him. "You are trying to live a faithful life and have devoted your time to being a man who helps others know the forgiveness of Christ. What more could a mother ask of her son but for him to believe that God's grace can make anything possible?"

He embraced her tightly and thanked God that throughout her life she had always had faith in him and had never stopped showing the love and mercy of Jesus.

Christmas Eve / Day
Luke 2:1-14 (15-20)

Welcoming God's Love

Kevin ignored the chiming from the computer and took a deep breath. He needed to be strong for his family. His little girl loved Christmas and everything about it so there was no way he was going to ruin that for her. He took another deep breath and clicked to connect. The screen filled with unruly curls and a smile that made his heart ache.

"Mommy," Cassidy shouted. "I can see Daddy!"

"I can see you too," he said. "We have a good connection this time."

Susan's face appeared as she settled Cassidy on her lap. He smiled and was rewarded with grins from both of them.

"Now, that is the reason I got up so early this morning."

Cassidy frowned. "Daddy, it's night time."

"Not here sweetie. Remember Daddy is in a different part of the world. The sun is already up here."

"Oh." Cassidy put her hands on her face. "I forgot."

"So what was your day like?"

"We finished putting up the stockings and went to church."

"Church?" Kevin asked in mock surprise. "It's not Sunday, is it?"

"Silly Daddy, its Christmas Eve. Baby Jesus gets born tomorrow." Cassidy giggled. "You're fooling with me."

"I am," he admitted. "So are you all ready for Christmas?"

"Are you coming home?"

"No sweetie, we talked about this." Kevin felt his chest tighten as he shook his head. "Daddy isn't able to come home for a couple more months."

"That long?"

He nodded trying to keep his face cheerful and upbeat.

"Are you ready for Baby Jesus?" Cassidy asked. "Do you have a tree up?"

"Of course," he said.

"Show me."

Kevin moved the camera so she could see around the communications tent. There was a tiny bush in the corner that one of the soldiers had decorated with red and green items they had found around camp.

"That's not as nice a tree as we have," she declared after examining it for a few moments. "But I like your angel."

"You've got good eyes." Kevin pointed at the tinfoil figure someone had stuck on a high branch.. "I hadn't noticed it."

"There are no presents underneath it," Cassidy said. "Where is the present we sent?"

"It is safe in my foot locker," he assured her. "I'll open it later today after breakfast."

"No Daddy, open it tomorrow after you sleep."

Kevin opened his mouth to start to explain about the international dateline when Susan piped up.

"That's what Daddy meant, sweetie."

"Oh," Cassidy bounded off her lap. "Don't go away I have something for you."

"Don't be long," Kevin said as she disappeared from sight. "I only have a couple more minutes on this call."

Tears welled up in Susan's eyes. "I miss you."

He touched his fingers to his lips and then to the screen. "Miss you too."

"How was yesterday?" She wiped at her face.

"Another day done before I can come home." Kevin thought of the mission report and debriefing. He pushed aside the sights and sounds which flashed through his memory. "How are you holding up?"

Susan smiled weakly. "The other families on base are good and the padre here is great with the kids. How's the padre there?"

"A nice man."

She sighed. "You haven't gone to services have you?"

"I don't see how a baby being born makes any difference in this world."

Susan's mouth tightened. "It was what Jesus did as an adult that makes the difference."

"I find it hard to have faith seeing what we see." Kevin held up his hand before she could respond. "I won't say anything to Cassidy. I know how important church and Christmas is to her."

"Kevin, it's Christmas. You should go to service." She touched the screen with her fingertips. "Think about it at least."

"I will." He forced a smile he knew she didn't believe. He intended to go straight back to his bunk, open his present, and get some shut eye before patrol. He noticed the timer turning red. "I am running out of time. Tell Cassidy that I love her and I'll call in two days at the same time."

Cassidy reappeared and threw herself onto her mother's lap. She held up a package she had obviously wrapped herself. "This is for you, Daddy."

"Sweetie, I already got your present. It came last week."

"This is a different present, Daddy. It's a Bible for when you come home," she said. "Because when you are hugging me I understand the stories about God's love."

Kevin choked out an "I love you" before the screen went blank. He stared at nothing for a few moments. He heard voices outside the tent and quickly wiped his eyes with his hand. People were heading toward the mess tent and he could hear the familiar strains of carols being sung. He put on his command face and headed for his bunk.

Part way there Kevin came to a halt. He couldn't stop seeing the Bible Cassidy held up and kept hearing her words. Kevin turned on his heel and marched into the worship service to join the singing. That Christmas morning when the padre read the story of God's love coming among us on earth Kevin opened his heart to the love his daughter knew when she was embraced by his arms.

Christmas 1
Luke 2:41-52

The Days after Christmas

Lucy finished her prayers and looked up at her mother. "I don't think I will go to church tomorrow morning."

"Why is that?"

"Well, I was thinking. I went at Christmas so I know the story of Jesus being born. I can also sing the words of the songs from memory."

"Yes, the music is very familiar this time of year." Her mother tucked her in. "But don't you like singing Christmas carols?"

"I do and I'm not going to stop singing them." Lucy yawned. "It's just that I already know the songs so I don't need to go to church to learn them."

"You know that church is about more than simply learning new things. It's also about thanking God."

"I already did that at Christmas. I was really excited because of all the presents I got and I said thank you for Jesus and for what was in my stocking, under the tree, and everything." Lucy paused and looked around her room. "But nothing new has happened since then so all I would be doing is saying the same thing over again. I don't want God to be bored with what I have to say so there is no need for me to go to church tomorrow."

Her mother looked at Lucy for a few moments and then kissed her forehead. She turned off the light but stopped before she closed the door. "What do you think will happen in the morning?"

"It will be the same as every other Sunday," Lucy said. "I will get up when my alarm rings and you'll make pancakes or something special for breakfast. Then we'll make sure all the dishes are done before it's time to leave for church."

"Okay." Her mother's brow furrowed for a moment. "Sleep tight and I will see you at seven."

The next morning Lucy woke to the familiar sounds of banging in the kitchen. She rolled out of bed and went down to see her mother putting a bowl and ingredients on the counter.

"Are we going to have pancakes for breakfast?" Lucy asked.

"I think we will. After all it is Sunday and that is what we do, isn't it?" Her mother smiled. "Are you up for them this morning?"

"Sure, I love it when you make pancakes."

Lucy helped her mother and before long they settled down to eat. Lucy enjoyed the pancakes and when it was time to clean up she got on her step stool and took the dishes after her mother washed them. They started telling jokes and Lucy was soon smiling and laughing.

"Oh, look at the time," her mother said. "I need to hurry to get ready for church. I can't wait to find out what is going to happen this morning. Plus I have something very important to be thankful for when we pray."

Lucy finished drying the dishes and looked all around the house. Everything was the same as far as she could tell. The tree with the unwrapped presents was still there and there was nothing new in any of the rooms she looked into. She thought for a long time and tried to remember everything that happened that morning. She couldn't think of anything that was different or out of the ordinary. Her mother came downstairs dressed in her Sunday best. She looked at Lucy for a moment, sighed, and headed for the door.

"Mom?" Lucy said. "Before you go I have a question."

"What is it?"

"Is there something in the house that I haven't seen? I mean is there a present that needs to be opened or something?"

"No," Her mother shook her head. "Everything is the same as it was Christmas Day."

"Did we do anything different this morning?"

"No, I think it was exactly what we do every Sunday before church."

"Oh." Lucy scratched her head. "Then what is it that you're so thankful about this morning?"

Her mother came over and hugged her. "I've had a wonderful week with you and am watching you grow up in front of me."

"I haven't grown any taller since Christmas," Lucy said.

"There are other ways to grow. In fact the Bible says that Jesus grew in wisdom and stature as a boy."

"What does wisdom and stature mean?"

"His mind and his body. I suspect it is going to be what the pastor will read in church this morning." Her mother looked at the clock. "Speaking of which, I should be leaving or I'm going to be late."

"Um." Lucy shuffled her feet. "I was thinking."

"Yes?"

"Maybe there are other things to be thankful for and reasons to go to church than just new things," Lucy said. "Can you wait for me to get ready?"

Her mother nodded, thankful that wisdom can be learned.

Christmas 2
John 1:(1-9) 10-18

Grace Filled

"The most important thing is knowing and understanding the law," the chief justice said without enthusiasm. His eyes scanned the gathered group of law enforcement and criminal justice experts tasked with trying to reform a system they all knew was broken. He had already heard from most of them and while everyone was able to point out what was wrong the weeks of hearings had produced little that would change things for the better. Honestly he was bored and wanted to go home.

"Judge, I'm not disagreeing that knowing and understanding the law is important," the lawyer in front of the podium said. "I am just saying that is not the only thing that is important. I wish more of you judges understood that."

The chief justice waved his hand in dismissal. "You are just upset because I usually rule against you when you appear before me."

"Of course I am upset at those times," the lawyer admitted.

"Then you have made my point." The chief justice shuffled some of the paper in front of him and wondered if anyone would notice if he stopped the proceedings early today.

"Judge, I'm not upset because you rule against me but because you don't listen to me."

"I don't need to listen to you when I know you are wrong or when the evidence shows your client is guilty."

The chief justice's attention wandered back to the papers in front of him. Each submission basically said the same thing. The legal system in this area was not helping people and probably making things worse because of how it treated the accused. The chief justice looked at his watch. "Did you have anything else to add?"

"I think a number of the problems could be fixed quite easily."

"So what is your solution? More money to hire additional judges or more money to hire extra support staff?" The chief justice held up the papers before him. "There is no money to do either."

"While both would be nice I think the problem is something that is more basic." The lawyer took a deep breath. "Can I speak frankly before you without my future clients suffering for it?"

The chief justice took off his reading glasses. "You've been appearing before me for almost twenty years. Have you not always found me to be a fair man?"

The lawyer nodded. "Yes, judge you are always fair. You may not like what I have to say though."

The chief justice closed the file folder in front of him. "Honestly, I have spent too long hearing the same things over and over so I am open to pretty much anything at this point."

The lawyer took another deep breath. "You need more people like Judge Johnson sitting on the bench."

"Judge Johnson?" The chief justice leaned forward. "He ruled against you the last three times you were before him, didn't he?"

"I lose before him more often than I do before you," the lawyer admitted. "However I would much prefer to argue a case in front of him."

"For heaven's sakes, why?"

"He listens when I make my case. He makes sure I have the time I need to mount a defense and lets me do the best that I can."

The chief justice stroked his chin. "Judge Johnson does take his time on occasion."

"Yet have you ever looked and see how often anyone appeals his rulings?"

The chief justice looked to his assistant. She typed into her laptop for a few moments and then handed him a slip of paper. He looked at the figures and wished the cases he heard were appealed that infrequently. His eyes went wide when he saw how few of Judge Johnson's rulings were actually overturned. The chief justice sat up in his seat and scanned the group. There was a good collection of lawyers in the room.

"Be honest now, how many of you are pleased when your case gets assigned to him?"

Most of the hands in the room shot up. The chief justice turned his attention back to the lawyer in front of him.

"So you are saying more time to make your case is the answer?"

"In part," the lawyer said, "fundamentally though it is the fact that he listens to us. My clients always feel like they are able to say what they need to say, that he sees them as people who deserve to be treated fairly no matter what they have done."

"Is there more than just the way he manages his court?"

"Even in his written rulings Judge Johnson is respectful in a way that honestly, Judge, I don't always feel for my clients." A ripple of laughter went through the group.

The chief justice smiled and sat back in his chair. He remembered something he heard in church about grace being under compassion and love. He wondered how he could inspire and encourage that within a system that dealt with justice and evil. The chief justice started scribbling notes feeling an optimism he had not felt in years as he thought about how he could change himself in order to make things better for the people around him.

32

New Year's Day
Matthew 25:31-46

Whatever You Do

Judy looked up from the table. "Who are those for?"

Marge packed the groceries on the counter into a cloth bag. She made sure it wasn't too heavy and then set it beside the door. "That is our weekly donation to the food bank. The church collects each Sunday and I like to make sure that we add something."

"It doesn't make any difference you know," Judy said. "The food bank has been around a long time and a couple cans of soup won't change anything."

"Maybe soup alone won't but some crackers, canned vegetables, and fruit should help someone make ends meet." Marge nodded her head toward the bag she had packed. "There is also spaghetti and sauce."

Judy frowned. "You know what I mean. You can't fight the causes of poverty with donations of food."

Marge shrugged. "Maybe not but I can help someone through the day at least. With a full stomach they have a better chance of changing their lives than with an empty one."

"You're assuming they want to change their lives and don't enjoy living on handouts."

"I can't imagine that anyone prefers to live day to day not knowing where their next meal comes from." Marge reached for an empty box and started filling it with clothes from a hamper.

"Why are you putting your laundry in boxes?"

"These are clothes we're not using or that the kids have outgrown." Marge placed a second box up on the counter.

"I suppose you are giving them away to the poor too."

Marge stopped what she was doing. "What else would I do with them?"

"You could sell them in a consignment shop."

Marge resumed sorting the clothes. "I'd prefer someone to have them who needs them."

"You are such a softy." Judy shook her head. "You give to everyone and everything."

"Thank you."

"I didn't mean it as a compliment."

"I know but I took it as one anyway." Marge smiled. "I do whatever I can to help out."

Judy looked at the accumulation of bags and boxes at the door. "Is all that going to charity?"

"Most of it. The bag is for the food bank at the church, the boxes will go to the clothing depot on the other side of town." Marge stacked the boxes together and pulled out a smaller cloth bag and began filling it with books.

"So I suppose those books are going somewhere as well?"

"Yes, I'm donating them to the prison. They have a library that inmates can borrow from when they want something to read."

"If you do the crime you should do the time." Judy scowled. "They shouldn't be coddled."

Marge held up the books on carpentry and auto repair than she was putting in the bag. "I wasn't aware that getting an education and learning was coddling."

"You know what I mean." Judy pointed at the bags and boxes by the door. "You know you could sell this stuff and make some money from it."

"I understand that." Marge put more books into the bag. "I prefer to give it away because I know it helps people who need it."

34

"You're giving to the hungry, the homeless, and to prisoners. You know none of them will appreciate it."

"I don't do it to have them appreciate me." Marge pulled out another cloth bag and began filling it with baby clothes.

"What is this for? Some other charity?"

"No, but I am giving them to someone I know needs them." She paused for a moment to smile. "I remember what it is like when your first child arrives and they are growing out of everything as fast as possible."

"Marge, no one will care what you do with those clothes," Judy said. "The person who receives them will just take them and not give a second thought about where they came from."

"If they don't, they don't."

"I don't know why you bother if no one cares."

Marge put the bag of baby clothes in front of her. "Pass these on to Cynthia and tell her to bring that grandchild of yours around whenever she is in this end of town, will you?"

Judy looked at the bag and her eyes filled with tears. "I don't know what to say."

"You don't have to say anything."

"These will help her out more than you can know."

Judy got up and put her arms around Marge. "Tell me what I can do to thank you."

"You don't have to do anything," Marge said, "but if you wanted to help me deliver these donations I could use a hand."

Judy started grabbing bags. "Let's swing by my house. I think I have some things to add to them."

Epiphany of Our Lord
Matthew 2:1-12

Find the Light

John sat in the back pew and watched as people came through the doors of the old country church. Greetings and best wishes were exchanged when familiar faces passed his seat. There was a sprinkling of young families and a few children in the congregation but most of the people had gray hair. John smiled as he thought of the Sundays he had sat with his family in this pew. He could still taste the peppermints his grandfather would give him when the pastor went into the pulpit to preach.

"Is this seat taken?" A young man dressed in an ill-fitting suit stood at the end of the row.

John slid down in the pew and introduced himself.

"Are you any relation to Charlie Adams?" the young man asked. "You look like him."

"Thank you. I'm his grandson."

"I'm Theodore. We would be related through your grandfather's sister, Alice. She was my mother's grandmother." Theodore chuckled. "Of course pretty much everyone here is a relative, aren't they?"

"The joys of a small country church. If you aren't related then you are neighbors."

"Too true. Makes me miss the city," Theodore said. "The church I go to there is ten times the size of this one and has two pastors."

"I've been to churches in cities that sat thousands of people and had multiple teams of pastors." John smiled. "Don't overlook the value of this church just because it is small and you know everyone."

"I guess so." Theodore looked doubtful. "I never met your grandfather but he is a real legend in this community."

"He was a great man. He used to take me to this church when I was a boy."

"I'm here for the holidays visiting my mother." Theodore nodded toward the front. "She's over there in the choir."

John couldn't help but notice the woman looking down with pride at the young man sitting next to him. "Are you in the city for university or work?

"University. I'm in my second year of engineering."

John looked at his seat mate more closely. "How's it going?"

"Great."

"Really?" John's locked eyes with him. "I know the program is a hard one."

"It's a lot of work." Theodore squirmed a bit. "I'm doing okay."

"Is it the workload or the fact that your friends who are in other subjects seem to have so much more free time on their hands?"

"Both." Theodore sighed. "Sometimes I wonder if it's all worth it."

"The journey is a long one to make but it can be rewarding." John tapped his professional engineering ring on the seat beside him. "Just remember what's important."

"What if you don't know what's important?"

"Then keep your eye fixed on the signs God gives to you." John pulled out a business card and handed it to him. "When you graduate give me a call if you are interested in an interview."

Theodore's eyes went wide when he saw the name of the prestigious engineering firm.

The opening chords of the first hymn began and they stood with the rest of the congregation. The hymns were old favorites of the season and everyone sang enthusiastically. The familiar story of the wise men was read from the large pulpit Bible by a girl who stumbled over some of the words. The pastor preached and there were some prayers. Then before John knew it the service of worship was over. He stayed in his seat and let the postlude and memories wash over him. When the music finished he noticed that only he and Theodore remained in the church.

"You have a good term at school." John rested his hand on Theodore's shoulder. "I am serious about you calling me if you want an interview when you graduate."

"Thank you, I certainly will." Theodore cleared his throat. "Can I ask you a question?"

John nodded. "Of course."

"Why do you come back here?" Theodore held up the business card. "You could go anywhere and if what I have heard is true you have been everywhere. What brings you back to this church?"

"When my grandfather brought me to this church I found what I needed here in these pews. No matter where I go and no matter what I do I usually find myself coming back."

"What could you have possibly found here?" Theodore looked around. "There isn't much in this little community. I mean you must have been in more impressive buildings, heard better choirs, listened to incredible preachers. What brings you back to this small unimportant church?"

John smiled. "This is the place I found Jesus."

Baptism of Our Lord
Luke 3:15-17, 21-22

Expectations

James closed his eyes and pretended to be asleep when Vera came into the room.

"Wake up," she said. "I need you to watch Vincent while I finish getting ready."

He sat up as his infant son was thrust into his arms. The little boy gurgled and gave him a big smile.

"Sure, you're happy," James whispered. "You get to sleep and eat while the rest of us have to sit in uncomfortable clothes listening to some boring preacher talk about something no one cares about."

His son squinted at him and then laughed. James shook his head, which made Vincent laugh all the more.

"I'll just be a few minutes longer," Vera called out from the bathroom. "You seem to have tickled his funny bone this morning."

"We're doing great in here." James looked at the clock and did some quick calculations. If Vera didn't leave him enough time to get ready then it would be her fault that he missed church. "No need to rush."

She reappeared and took Vincent back. "Don't worry. You've got plenty of time to get ready."

"I guess so." James slowly got out of bed.

"Your son is being baptized and all my family will be there. We need to leave by ten at the latest." Vera swept out of the room.

James grumbled as he got dressed. This was the one day of the week when he didn't have to work either at the office or at home. He resented having to waste half of it at church. Vera was waiting for him at the front door. She didn't say anything but her foot was tapping ever so slightly and the clock showed just past ten. As they drove down the quiet streets, James wished he had never agreed to go to church. They took the last space in the nearby parking lot.

"I'm going to find the pastor. They have reserved seats for us near the front." Vera frowned. "One Sunday morning in church isn't going to hurt you, you know."

He held up his hands. "Have I said anything?"

She shook her head and disappeared inside. James took his time getting up the stairs. He gave a faint smile at the ushers who handed him a bulletin. There was a gathering for fathers and their children that coming Saturday. He hoped Vera didn't see it. The last thing he wanted was her pestering him to spend more time in church.

"Hey, James!"

"Phil!" James extended his hand to his friend and neighbor. "It's nice to see a familiar face."

"Vera told me it's a special day." Phil grinned. "I'm thrilled to be here for Vincent's baptism."

"Really?"

"Absolutely. I wouldn't have missed it for the world."

"Thanks. Sorry you had to give up a Sunday morning."

"What else is Sunday morning for but church?" Phil asked.

"I can think of a few things," James said. "Football, sleeping, reading..."

Phil waved his hand. "You can do those things any other time in the week. It's not too much to set aside some time to spend with God."

"Did Vera put you up to saying that?"

"Not in the least. Truth is when my boys were born I decided that I wanted to be a better man for them." Phil looked around at the church. "There is no better place to do that than here. After all who better than our Father in heaven to help us be good fathers here on earth?"

Phil clasped him on the shoulder and then headed off to rejoin his family. James made his way to the reserved seats and sat next to Vera. He only half listened as the service started because he was thinking about what Phil said. He looked at his son. James did want to be a good father. He looked at his wife. He wanted to be a better husband as well.

When the time came for the baptism, he went forward with Vera and paid attention as the pastor asked them how they would raise Vincent. James promised to raise him in the Christian faith and realized as the words passed his lips that he meant it. He wanted to be the best he could be for his son and knew that Vera was right about them coming to church. When they returned to their seats, he found himself interested and engaged in the rest of the service.

Vera gathered up Vincent and started toward the door after the pastor pronounced the blessing. "Thanks for being patient through the service. We can go now."

James looked over at a crowd heading for coffee and fellowship. "I think I want to talk to Phil and maybe the pastor."

"Really?"

"Yes." James took Vincent into his arms. "Really."

James had no doubt he was heading in the direction he was supposed to go in his life as he walked with his wife and son further into the church.

Epiphany 2
John 2:1-11

What Comes Next?

The machines buzzed and beeped at regular intervals but Hazel's eyes were firmly fixed on the open door of her hospital room. She relaxed when Simon entered and sat beside her.

"I'm dying you know."

His face tightened. "Mom, don't say things like that."

"It's true." She reached out her hand to him. "I am an old woman and my time is drawing near."

"Mom, the medicine might…"

"…nothing is going to change the fact that I am not long for this world." She squeezed his hand. "I love you."

Simon's eyes filled with tears. "I love you too."

"Good, then I need you to listen to me." She drew a deep breath. "I was raised by two incredible parents. They provided me with a loving home and encouraged me to be the best person possible. Those days on the farm are treasured memories I still hold to this day."

"Grandpa and Grandma were special people."

"They were." Hazel closed her eyes picturing their faces.

Simon cleared his throat. "We don't have to do this now, Mom."

"Yes, we do." She opened her eyes and looked into his. "I thought my life was great but when I met your father things got even better. He was charming, witty, and loved me without hesitation. One of the happiest days of my life was when we got married in the small country church."

"I remember the story."

"Yet I was even happier when you were born." Hazel smiled. "I thank God to this day that I have such a wonderful son. You were there for me through your father's illness and every day during these last twelve years. Thank you."
A tear ran down Simon's cheek. "I wish I could do more."
"You have done everything a mother could want." Hazel struggled to keep her eyes open. "You need to call my grandchildren now because I want to speak with them."
"Okay. Rest now, Mom." Simon held Hazel's hand until her breathing became regular and even. Then he went outside to the hallway and made some phone calls.
Hazel opened her eyes to see Simon sitting with Mary and their two children.
"Good, you are all here so I can continue." She took a deep breath. "I thought Simon was the pride of my life but when he met you Mary my life became richer because I gained a wonderful daughter."
Mary leaned forward and kissed Hazel on the forehead. "I love you, Mom"
"I love you too, Mary." Hazel took her daughter-in-law's hand. "You have been a friend and a rock for me. The day Simon married you I thought my life couldn't get any better."
Hazel held her hand for a few more moments and then let go. "John and Sarah come closer."
Her grandchildren went to the other side of the bed and Hazel turned her head toward them. "You don't remember your grandfather because he died before you were born. Your mother and father were always there for me and I feel richly blessed because of them. "
Hazel struggled to catch her breath.
"Nana, you need to rest," John said softly.
She shook her head. "I'll have time enough to rest soon. John, when you were born your parents were so excited and proud. What they didn't know was that I was surprised."

John looked over at his parents who shrugged their shoulders.

"I was surprised because I thought my life as a widow was only going to be a pale shadow of what it had been like when your grandfather was alive. Yet with you and then Sarah in my world things got exciting, busy, and joyful again." Hazel reached out her hand and took his. "You are my pride and joy. A fine young man who has made his way in the world and are starting to really shine."

"Thanks Nana." John's voice was a whisper. "I love you."

"I love you too. Now move over and let your sister talk to me."

Everyone chuckled as Sarah pushed in next to John. Hazel took her hand.

"Sarah, you haven't yet found out what your life is going to be like because you're still young." Hazel smiled at her. "Don't worry about your future because I know that you will do wonderful things."

"I hope so, Nana," Sarah said.

"I know so because you are also my pride and joy. You're kind and smart and anything you decide to do you can do." Hazel squeezed her hand. "I love you."

Sarah wiped her face with her sleeve. "I love you too."

"I know that my time is not long in this world and I want you to know that I thank God for richly blessing me. I had great parents, a loving husband, a wonderful son and daughter-in-law, and terrific grandchildren. Even when times were hard I found that God gave me something new and incredible to experience in life." Hazel fell into a coughing fit.

Simon stepped close to the bed. "Mom, you need to rest."

"What I need to tell you is one last thing. Something important for each of you to always remember." Hazel took a deep breath and said her final words on earth. "God always saves the best for last."

Epiphany 3
Luke 4:14-21

Seeing the Kingdom

Kevin sat in the church listening as the pastor spoke of Jesus proclaiming that the scriptures had come true in the presence of the people listening to him. His pulse raced as he imagined the scene in the synagogue that morning. How thrilling it would have been to be there. How exciting to know God was at work. How great a blessing to see miracles and lives changing in front of your eyes. The excitement lasted through the rousing hymn they sang and the prayers that they prayed for the Holy Spirit to be among them.

When the benediction was pronounced Kevin felt a bit of disappointment as the congregation dispersed. The excitement of hearing that God was at work began to fade as he thought of all the problems in the world. He wished it was as easy to think of ways that God was helping those in need.

Kevin noticed Jane making her way to the exit with her cane and held the door for her.

"Thank you, Kevin."

Kevin helped her down the stairs to the sidewalk. "How are you doing today? Do you need me to walk you to your car?"

"No, Martha is here to pick me up so I'll be fine." She smiled. "It's taking some time but I am getting around better now, thanks."

Kevin watched her slowly make her way to the waiting car and thought to himself that Jane was someone who could definitely use scripture being fulfilled in her life. She had spent months in the hospital after her heart attack and was only now starting to get out and around. He knew because he had delivered meals to her with the others in the men's group and been a link in the prayer chain that prayed for her.

"It is great to see Jane in church again, isn't it?" Charles asked from beside him.

Kevin nodded. "The church is richer with her among us."

"That's for sure," Charles said. "Are you still able to come to the meeting on Tuesday night?"

"I wouldn't miss it for the world." Kevin clasped Charles on the shoulder. "One year is a big anniversary."

"Thanks." Charles beamed from ear to ear. "You've always been there for me. I know I wasn't always that great a friend when I was lost in a bottle."

"Hey, you're not that person anymore."

Charles frowned. "Sometimes it's hard to not have a drink."

"Which is why you have a sponsor and the group for support."

"Some nights I do nothing but pray for God to help me."

"Hey." Kevin squeezed his shoulder. "You've made it through the first year. Now all you have to do is rack up a few more – 7:30, right?"

Charles' smiled returned. "I'll save you a seat."

Kevin watched his friend head off and thought to himself that Charles could definitely use scripture being fulfilled in his life. He had been a mess and was only now starting to sort things out. Susan had begun to talk to him again and while their marriage was probably beyond repair, Kevin hoped for the sake of the kids they could be civil at least.

Kevin saw Mun-jan coming out the door and dipped his head slightly. "How are you this day, my friend?"

Mun-jan bowed in response. "I am pleased to be in such a wonderful country as this one. So much freedom and the chance to come to worship without worrying about the secret police."

Kevin whistled softly. "You really had to fear being arrested for going to church?"

"That and worse. I am blessed to be in this country where there are so many freedoms."

"This is a great land to live in," Kevin agreed.

"I am also humbled to have a wonderful church in this land helping me become a citizen."

"It is we who are richer because of your presence among us."

Mun-jan bowed deeply. "You honor me yet again. I do not wish to impose but do you have time to have coffee?"

Kevin looked at his watch. "Sure I can have a cup with you."

The man grinned. "That is wonderful because I am excited to practice English with you. I will join you downstairs?"

"Certainly." Kevin watched as the former refugee went back into the church.

Mun-jan could definitely stand seeing a miracle in his life. After all the man had been forced to flee from a terrible oppressive land and the story he had shared of his escape was filled with so much difficulty and turmoil.

Kevin made his way inside the church thinking about Jesus preaching in the synagogue and wished again that he could see scripture being fulfilled in his sight. He wanted so much to know that God heard and helped those who were in physical pain, in spiritual need, and who were persecuted. He didn't think that would ever happen yet he couldn't shake the feeling that he was missing something taking place right before his eyes.

Epiphany 4
Luke 4:21-30

Unwelcome Words

First Church traced its history to the initial settlers of the town who met in a house to worship. That fledgling congregation built a small hall in which to gather for service and study. Soon that building was overflowing with people so a proper church was built next to the hall. Each time the town expanded so did First Church in both people and buildings.

Some of that was because First Church was the place to attend. They were trendsetters when it came to music, production quality of their services, and in investing their growing financial endowments. The congregation was also proud to say their church was active seven days a week. The building was used each and every day for church fellowship and study groups. First Church had full pews, a rich history, a healthy bank account, and was envied by churches in the surrounding towns.

It was a bit of a surprise when a renowned evangelist known for his passionate preaching for Christ refused their invitation to come and speak. There had been some debate over whether or not he should be invited since some thought he wasn't exactly First Church material. However when the Board heard that he was coming to their town they decided if he was speaking anywhere he was coming to First Church. They offered him the use of their facility. He politely refused. They repeated the offer thinking that perhaps he did not understood the opportunity they were offering to him. He repeated his refusal.

A few took this to mean he was not worth their attention. If he wasn't going to be speaking at First Church why pay any attention to him? Others were upset and suggested that everyone boycott his service. If he rejected them why shouldn't they reject him? Most people though were confused that he would choose to speak in a field rather than at their historic and prestigious church. Why wasn't he speaking about the gospel in a church so richly blessed?

The day came for the evangelist to arrive and everyone gathered to hear him speak. Some came because they were curious and a few because they were interested in what he had to say but most attended because they wanted to know how he could possibly snub First Church.

The service in the field began with some prayers and hymns. Then the evangelist read the passage from Luke about Jesus preaching in his hometown. There was a rustle in the crowd as the people from First Church knew that Jesus had not been well received in the synagogue that day. Yet as the evangelist began to speak he described the mission of the church to bring the good news to the world. The people at First Church thought of how much others envied their building, weekly attendance, and budget, and they decided that the evangelist was probably not as bad as they had assumed. After all he was basically telling them that they were doing everything right.

That was until the evangelist started talking about the need for people of faith to understand that God was also at work beyond the walls of their buildings. With those words, the people of First Church became restless. When the evangelist suggested that the measure of a church's success was not money or how many people sat in the pews each Sunday but rather faithfulness, they began to murmur among themselves. How dare he suggest that they, with all their history, endowments, and great presence in the town were not the place through which God acted? After all they had everything they needed and wanted.

Then the evangelist said that it was easy for people of faith to make idols out of their buildings and bank accounts. He claimed that all too often churches value them more than they value following Christ. At that point the people of First Church had heard enough. They began to shout at the evangelist and accused him of being a fraud and a thief. They threw things at him and forced him to flee for his life.

The people of First Church went back to their beautiful building, great endowments, and all the other things they treasured. They congratulated themselves for stopping that terrible preacher from speaking his slander in their town.

However some of the people who were there at the field that day stopped going to First Church and met instead at a house on Sunday mornings. They read the Bible and devoted themselves to discovering what Christ was calling them to do in their lives. They planned an effort to reach into the community rather than wait for the community to come to them. For despite what some people wanted the Spirit was still at work in the town.

Epiphany 5
Luke 5:1-11

Unexpected Blessings

Robert valued hard work. He always arrived early, gave his full attention to the task at hand and persevered until it was successfully completed. There were many ways in which Robert did not live up to his potential. He was short-tempered, broke his word when it suited him, and had a selfish nature that he indulged. Yet when it came to work Robert let nothing stop him from doing his best. The skill of his hands and the focus of his mind were treasures he refused to squander.

One day because he was unhappy with the quality of the water he was getting, Robert set about digging a new well for his house. He rented all the equipment, chose the most likely spot in his yard, and began to dig. He worked hard until sunset but did not strike water.

The next day he spent time consulting locals about where the water tables were in the area, examined local maps, and then went back to work digging. He dug holes all morning and all afternoon in the most likely spots, yet he still did not strike water.

The third day he went back over all the material he had gathered about water on his property. He looked at where he had preciously dug and how deep he had gone and tried again to find water. He had no success. He had a yard full of test holes that had been dug and filled back in, a mountain of notes and maps about where water should be on his property, but no well that would give him what he wanted. When

51

evening came he went to sleep wondering if he would ever find water.

That night he dreamed that he was looking at his property. He looked at each hole he had dug and saw that they were dry. He began to despair that he would never have a well to give him water. Then he heard a voice saying "try again in the first place you dug." He woke to find the sun shining and a new day beginning.

At breakfast, he thought about the dream and the voice telling him where to dig and dismissed it as wishful thinking. He re-examined all the material that he had about water in the area. He reviewed the wisdom of the locals and a map showing where he had already tried looking for water. He went outside and spent the day desperately searching in new locations with no success. As the daylight began to fade he headed back to the house and passed by the initial hole he dug on that first day.

He paused for a moment and then, because he really had nothing to lose and because he hated leaving a job unfinished, he began to dig. He felt foolish as he moved earth that had already been moved. He worked without much enthusiasm and was just about to stop when he heard the sound of rushing water.

He was astounded to see a stream of water bubbling up from the ground. He took some in his hand and tasted the most clear, crisp water that had ever passed his lips. He rejoiced at a job well done and stepped back to admire his handiwork. All of which caused him to think about the dream. Part of him wanted to dismiss it as simply a coincidence or as his subconscious helping him solve the problem. Yet he knew he dug no deeper to find water than he had on that first day when the well produced nothing. He had no rational explanation for why there was plenty of water flowing from a hole that should be dry.

Robert thought about it as he cleaned and put away the equipment and could not shake the feeling that something important had happened in his life. Robert now believed there was a God and that changed everything for him. He wasn't holy by anyone's definition yet he felt that something miraculous happened when the voice spoke to him in the dream. He had no idea why God would speak to him but he knew he had to do something in response.

The next morning when Robert woke he decided to take a day off work and head toward a church to speak to the pastor about prayer. He knew he was not the best person but assumed that if God had spoken to him then it was appropriate for him to learn how to speak with God.

Epiphany 6
Luke 6:17-26

Acceptable to God

There once was a land where some people had plenty and wanted for nothing. They owned fields and had water for their animals. They lived in homes with many comforts and always had plenty of food and riches when the inevitable problems of the world arose. Life was good for these people and they greeted each other with warm smiles and invitations to feasts and celebrations. They considered themselves fortunate, blessed, and the best people of the land. They believed that God was with them in their prosperity so they went to church and gave thanks that they were not like those who did not have plenty.

For within the land there were others who lived a much different life. Those people had very little. They had no fields of their own and either worked for others or lived in areas where no people should have to live. They stayed in ramshackle homes that were overcrowded and dangerous because there was no other place for them in the land. Life was hard for those people. There was never enough food for the day and worries about tomorrow filled their hearts. They went around with their heads lowered because they were ashamed to look at each other. There were no feasts or celebrations for them to enjoy. Their idea of a blessing was simply a day where things had not become worse in their lives. When they went to church and saw those who had plenty they wondered why the world was so unfair and what they had done to deserve their fates. They prayed that their lives might change and asked God to save them.

One day at church, that one place where those who had plenty gathered with those who had nothing, a stranger stood in the pulpit. He looked at those who had nothing and said "Blessed are you for God sees what is happening. Know that things will change."

He looked at those who had plenty. "Woe to you for God sees what is happening in this land. Know that things will change." The stranger then disappeared in a flash of light.

All the people, both those who had plenty and those who had nothing, sat in stunned silence. They were amazed that God had chosen to speak to them and felt humbled that they had heard a message from the divine in their lives. That was until they started to think about what the man had said. Then the church erupted in chaos as the people tried to make sense of the words.

Some of those who had nothing could not believe what the messenger had said. Surely the man, if he was indeed from God, knew that they lived terrible lives. If God blessed them why did they not have the riches of those who had plenty? They shook their heads and slunk back to their lives.

A few of the people who had nothing though rejoiced in their hearts that God had heard their prayers and was with them. They left filled with hope and their heads held high.

There was also a split among those who had plenty. Some dismissed the man as a fraud. After all he had said God was with those who had nothing but everyone knew that God was on their side because they possessed great riches. They left shaking their heads at such folly.

A few of the people who had plenty though heard the message and considered what it meant for their lives. For the first time they began to wonder if what they had, the wealth they enjoyed, was not simply meant to enrich their lives and those who were like them. They left with eyes seeing a different vision of the world and minds considering a whole new way of life.

In the days that followed those who had plenty and rejected the message continued to believe that their wealth was only for them and they began to fear those who had nothing. Those who had nothing and rejected the message continued to suffer and despair at life and how nothing ever changed for them.

Yet life was different for those who heard and accepted the message of the stranger that day. Their lives were changed from the moment they believed that God expected more from them than how they had been living. The people who had plenty opened their hands to those who had nothing. Those who had nothing embraced the opportunities offered to them and shared freely their own faith and abilities. Together the transformed people saw the riches and opportunities of the land as a gift for the community and devoted themselves to working for the greater good of all. For they no longer saw anyone as wealthy or poor but rather understood that they were all sisters and brothers in God's kingdom.

Epiphany 7
Luke 6:27-38

Like the Most High

Kevin followed Lateasia out of the school into the parking lot.

"Why do you do that?" he asked.

"Do what?"

"Be nice to Shaun." Kevin looked back at the closed doors behind him. "He doesn't like you. I wouldn't give him the time of day."

"I know." Lateasia waited for him to catch up. "That's just who I am."

"It's lame and you need to stop it." Kevin pointed to where he was parked.

"Why?"

"He is taking advantage of you." Kevin stopped next to his car. "He didn't need to borrow your notes."

"He was sick yesterday."

"He was skipping. I heard him boast about it to his friends."

"He still missed the class." Lateasia shifted her book bag to the other shoulder. "He needs to catch up and I don't mind lending him my notes."

"You should mind. He isn't your friend at all." Kevin threw up his hands. "Did you know he talks about you behind your back?"

"Yeah, I do." Lateasia looked down. "I came around the corner one day and he was saying how lame he thought I was."

"Did he even have the decency to be embarrassed when you caught him?"

"No." She looked at Kevin. "He just stared for a moment and then laughed."

"That was beyond cruel." Kevin clenched his fists.

Lateasia reached over and touched his arm. "It's okay."

"No, it's not okay. Don't you even care that he is mean to you one moment and then all sweet and nice to you when he wants something?"

"Sure. I wish he was a better person, I really do." Lateasia shrugged. "But he isn't, so I have to take him as he is."

"Why?"

"Because until he changes that's who he is."

"I thought you were a woman who believed in standing up for your rights." Kevin's eyes went to the environmental and social justice stickers on her book bag.

"I am." She followed his gaze. "I believe we should work for justice here at home and around the world."

"So you are okay with standing up against evil in other places but roll over when you face it in your own life?"

She shook her head. "Completely different things. I never do anything for Shaun that I do not want to. I am choosing to be nice to him."

"I know. That is why I think you are crazy. Why would you be nice to someone who is miserable to you?"

She fingered the cross around her neck. "It's what I believe I am supposed to do."

"I don't get it." Kevin rubbed his forehead. "What does being nice to Shaun because he is two-faced and mean have to do with faith?"

"It shows love."

"Lateasia, you are one of the most loving people I know. You are patient with your little brother, a good friend to most of the kids at school, and polite and kind to everyone else."

Kevin sighed. "I don't know how anyone could expect you to be more loving that you are."

"Jesus said for us to love our enemies and do good to those who persecute us."

"That is why I don't go to church." Kevin took out his car keys and unlocked the door. "I can't believe in a God who would ask me to do that."

"Jesus asks us to do that because that is how God loves us." Lateasia reached over and took his hand.

Kevin's brow furrowed. "Okay. Now you have lost me. What does one have to do with the other?"

"I used to hate God and the church."

Kevin's jaw dropped. "You?"

"Yes, me. When my parents were killed in that car accident I stopped going to church. I hated God for what happened." Tears filled her eyes. "I didn't cry, I got angry."

"You were just a kid." Kevin squeezed her hand. "No one could blame you for being upset like that."

"That's the point. God kept loving me even though I screamed at the walls at night saying how much I hated him." Lateasia wiped her face with her free hand. "One time when I thought I couldn't take it anymore I found myself praying like my mom had taught me and that is when it happened."

Kevin stood very still "What?"

"I felt the love and care of God. It was like there was someone in my room holding me as I cried and cried." She smiled. "That's when I understood those words you are having so much trouble hearing."

Kevin thought about it for a moment. "You've lost me again."

"Jesus loves us even when we hate Jesus. Jesus offers salvation not because we love him but because he loves us so much." She held Kevin's hand tightly. "And that is the love he asks his followers to share with the world."

Epiphany 8
Luke 6:39-49

A Solid Foundation

Patricia handed Laura a tissue. "How are you doing?"
"I'm fine all things considered." Laura wiped her eyes. "I just needed a break from talking."
"I can understand that." Patricia looked out from the corner they were in at the people mingling and telling stories at the funeral reception. "This is all pretty overwhelming."
Laura sighed. "It is."
"You know you can come and stay with me for a few weeks." Patricia turned her attention back to her sister. "I would love the company."
Laura shook her head. "I think I'm still going to fly out tomorrow afternoon."
"I thought you had an open ticket."
"I do."
"Then why the big rush to get back?" Patricia asked. "You said you were off work until the start of next month."
"It hurts too much." Laura's eyes brimmed over with tears. "I've lost my best friend in the world."
Patricia held her and they both wept. She handed Laura another tissue when her sobbing subsided.
Laura blew her nose. "I don't know how you can do it."
"Do what?"
"Be so calm through all of this," Laura said. "Why aren't you torn up inside?"
"Sis, I don't know what you are thinking but I lost my mother too. These past few days have been the hardest of my life."

"It doesn't seem like it." Laura pointed at the people looking at pictures arranged at the other end of the church hall. "You were over there laughing a few moments ago with Mom's friends."

"I was," Patricia admitted. "They reminded me about the time Mom went on the cruise with them and ended up winning the limbo contest."

A big smile flashed across Laura's face and then disappeared in a scowl. "This isn't a time for joy."

"Why not?" Patricia reached out and took Laura's hand. "Mom is at peace."

"She's gone." Tears flowed down Laura's face. "How can you be so calm about that?"

"Because I believe that Mom is in a better place and I know that she isn't suffering any more."

"She's dead."

"She is." Patricia took a deep breath. "I also know that death is a part of life. Mom knew that and she was ready. She knew Jesus loved her and would take her home to be with Daddy."

"I can't believe that," Laura whispered.

"Why not?" Patricia asked. "You were with Mom and me those final days. You heard her say those exact words. You know she believed and trusted in God."

Laura nodded. "She did."

"Then what's the problem?"

"I can't."

"You can't what?"

"I can't believe." Laura's face clouded over. "When I think about Mom all I feel is pain that she is gone."

Patricia put her arm around her. "I feel that loss too."

"No, you don't understand. That's all I feel." Laura looked at the program from the funeral. "Everything that we sang about at the service, everything the pastor read, and all that he spoke about didn't help me at all." Laura averted her eyes. "I haven't been to church in years. Maybe God doesn't care about me anymore."

"You know that's not true. God doesn't stop loving us even when we wander away."

"I know and I tried today to pray but every time I closed my eyes all I could do was feel that Mom was gone and my life was over." Laura wiped her cheeks. "It feels like my world has come crashing down."

Patricia pulled her sister close and held her for a few moments.

"I don't know what I am going to do," Laura said.

"Why don't you stay with me for a couple of days."

"Really?" Laura's eyes went wide. "After everything I have said you still would have me in your house?"

"Of course I would, we're family." Patricia hugged her. "Besides I think I might be able to help you put your life back together."

Laura looked at her for a few moments. "How?"

"Maybe you could come to church."

"It's been a long time."

"Never too late to start building your life over on a firm foundation," Patricia said. "There's a hymn sing on tomorrow night. Do you still love to sing?"

A smile touched her sister's face. "I think that would be nice. And Sis?"

"Yes?"

"Thanks for that." Laura kissed Patricia on the cheek.

"For what?"

"For helping me start over when I thought everything was finished."

"Heaven knows Mom did that enough for me," Patricia said. "I'm just following what she taught us about love and grace."

Transfiguration of Our Lord
Luke 9:28-36 (37-43)

The Experience of a Lifetime

Thomas found John watching the band do a sound check in the main hall. He sat down beside him and leaned over. "Having a good time?"

"The best." John's face lit up. "This youth conference is everything you said it would be."

"You sound like you didn't believe me."

"Thomas, I honestly didn't."

Thomas put his hand over his heart. "You're hurting me. Why wouldn't you believe your older brother?"

John rolled his eyes. "Maybe it started when you told me that Mrs. Wilson gave a lot of homework when I went into her second grade class."

"She does."

John shook his head. "You neglected to tell me that she gives plenty of time during the day to work on it."

Thomas scratched his head. "Did I forget to mention that fact?"

"Or maybe when you told me our neighbor was actually a spy or when you had me convinced that shampoo was made from…"

Thomas held up his hands. "Okay. I admit that I did tease you a bit when we were younger. But have I ever told you something that wasn't true when it was important?"

"No, I guess not." John rubbed his chin. "You were the one who was honest with me about what happened to Aunt Jolene and Uncle Carl."

"Then why would you doubt me about this?"

"Maybe because you really didn't say anything about what this weekend would be like other than 'Bro you really need to go cause you would love it.'"

"So how are you finding it?"

"It's well... the music... the preaching is..." John's eyes went wide. "I guess it is hard to put into words."

Thomas slumped back in his chair. "So now you see my problem. How do you explain an experience where you get to worship and learn with so many other teens from all over the country?"

John nodded. "Incredible for sure. Every bit of it has made me that much more excited about Jesus and my faith."

Thomas narrowed his eyes. "But?"

"Huh?"

"Come on, bro. I know that tone."

"It may seem stupid to say." John looked at the floor. "I guess I feel kind of sad too."

"You mean because you wish that every Sunday or church event could be like this?"

John's eyes went wide. "How did you know?"

"I felt the same way the first year I came." Thomas tapped his chin with his finger. "And I guess pretty much every other year too."

"Really?"

"Yeah." Thomas nodded. "This is a mountain top experience like the pastor spoke about in the morning service. We're here feeling the Holy Spirit moving and having our hearts and minds opened to Jesus and we don't want it to end."

"Tomorrow morning we have to go home."

"Exactly. Which means you are going to have to make a choice."

John tilted his head to one side. "What do you mean?"

"Some of the kids who attended the first year I came are still coming."

"Yeah, I've met some of them." John looked through the doors at the teens starting to arrive for the concert. "They are incredible people."

"They sure are. You didn't meet the people who attended and never came back."

"Huh?" John shifted in his chair to look at his brother. "Why wouldn't you come back if you had an experience like this?"

"I guess you go home and nothing measures up so you end up becoming disappointed that church and youth events aren't like this conference."

John thought for a moment. "I can see that. Our little youth group can't compare to this."

"No way it can with only a handful of kids."

"Huh? You've never seemed down on youth group before. You always encourage me to go."

"Why wouldn't I? It's a great group and the Darby's are good people."

John frowned. "You've lost me."

Thomas took a deep breath. "You've got a choice. You can take this great religious experience and then try to find more experiences like this and if things don't measure up then you can be down on them and wander away from church."

"Or?"

"Or you can take this great experience and use it to help make other experiences better." Thomas pointed toward the band members who were talking to each other. "You know that I picked up some of their music and we used them for worship on youth Sunday?"

John slapped his leg. "I knew that opening song yesterday sounded familiar!"

"Take what's happened here, give thanks to God, and then let God use this experience to help you make a difference out there." Thomas waved at the window.

John rubbed his chin. "So instead of leaving this place and trying to find another religious experience like this one you're saying God wants us to use this experience to bring Jesus to other people."

"I couldn't have said it better myself."

John rolled his eyes. "You're going to use those words when we report back to the congregation, aren't you?"

"No, I'm not." Thomas grinned at his brother. "You are."

Ash Wednesday
Matthew 6:1-6, 16-21

What Jesus Asks

Simone held the door for the elderly man. She sighed as he pushed past her with his bulging grocery bags.
"I think that is the last person," she said. "Are we finally done?"
"Seems like that time again." Ruth looked at the clock. "That was a busy morning, wasn't it?"
"It thought it would never end."
Ruth laughed. "Some days are like that. You want to lock up?"
Simone used her keys and then flipped the sign over to show the food bank was closed. "Do you need help finishing up the paperwork?"
"No, I'm fine." Ruth opened the laptop and started punching keys. "See you Thursday?"
"Sure." Simone grabbed her coat from behind the counter and headed toward the door.
"You know we did some great work this morning," Ruth called after her.
Simone waved good-bye without turning around. Ruth was always so upbeat at the end of their volunteer shift while Simone just wanted to crawl under a rock. All those people, all that need, and so much ingratitude.
She could count on one hand the people who said "thank you" since she started at the food bank six weeks ago. She couldn't believe the selfish attitude of the poor who came looking for help. Most complained about how long they had to wait or grumbled because there was something in the

package that they didn't want. She shook her head as she remembered the woman who complained about getting a chicken instead of a turkey in her Christmas hamper.

She kept thinking about how unfair it was all through Wednesday. The church was doing these people a great service. The least they could do was be grateful for it. They needed to recognize the hard work that volunteers like her put in. There were other things more enjoyable that Simone could be doing on Tuesday and Thursday mornings. She didn't appreciate having to deal with surly people who were never satisfied. Simone made up her mind that she was going to talk with Ruth and they were going to start making people thank them or they wouldn't receive any help.

When Simone arrived on Thursday morning there was already a crowd of needy people waiting for the food bank to open. Most had their heads down and wouldn't meet her gaze. A few tapped their watches and glared at her. Simone used her key to get in and slammed the door shut.

"Something the matter?" Ruth asked.

"We are doing a great service and helping people in need, aren't we?"

Ruth started counting bags in preparation for the morning's rush. "I believe we are."

"Doesn't the Bible tell us to have a grateful heart?"

"Absolutely."

Simone strode to the counter. "Then I think we should ask, no require, people say thank you when they get their food."

Ruth locked eyes with Simone. "Absolutely not."

Simone crossed her arms. "Why not?"

"Why are you here?"

"The pastor asked for volunteers one Sunday."

"Why did he do that?"

"Because this is a ministry of the church."

"So tell me, why do we do this?" Ruth gestured at the cans of food on the shelves and then at the people standing outside. "Why do we give out food to people who are desperate and needy, who are often angry and bitter?"

"Because Jesus asks us to."

"You ever wonder why Jesus asks us to care for these people?"

Simone paused and her arms fell to her sides. "They are important to him."

"He loves them and wants us to do the same. So we do this because of love. No other reason." Ruth came around the counter and touched her arm. "I know it can be discouraging and disheartening to not be thanked but that is not why we do this, Simone."

Simone frowned. "It wouldn't be that difficult for them to say thanks."

"We don't want to make things any harder for the people out there." Ruth gestured at the crowd. "Heaven knows most of the men and women who come here are using all their courage just to get through the door. I know it took every ounce of strength I had to ask for help when Charlie was sick."

Simone looked at the faces of the people waiting in line. She imagined how she would feel if she was standing there because she was hungry. "Okay."

Simone opened the door, went back to the counter, and started to hand out food. The morning passed quickly and before long the line was dwindling. Simone was tired when the last person left but she didn't feel discouraged. As each person came to get their food, she saw a brother and sister in need and reminded herself that we help family for no other reason but love.

Lent 1
Luke 4:1-13

Answering Temptation

Fred looked up at the cross hanging on the wall. He grew up in this congregation. His parents brought him here to be baptized and this was where he went to Sunday school. Fred was passionate about his Christian faith when he was in High School and attended regional youth programs and events. The Bible on his night stand was the one he received when he professed his faith in Jesus and joined the church.

He knew he had wandered away from his faith after graduation. In university, he only attended chapel when some of his friends were going or when there was a girl he wanted to impress. More often than not he slept in on Sunday mornings and used the time to catch up on work he needed to do before class on Monday.

He didn't return to church when he got his degree and started working in his hometown. It wasn't that he didn't believe or that he had anything against church. It wasn't that the woman he married didn't like church or didn't believe. He was just too busy and there always seemed to be something else that was more important for him to do. His Bible sat on the bookstand gathering dust and he prayed only when he was at a family reunion and someone asked him to say grace. Whenever he drove past a church he thought about God, he remembered how he used to read scripture every day, and he told himself that things really needed to change in his life. That commitment lasted until he reached the next block.

Fred shifted in the pew. He couldn't remember exactly what led him back to church. There was no specific event but a series of things that happened in his life. His mother got sick and he was comforted when the pastor came to pray with her in the hospital. He clicked on a link that his friend had sent him about a new translation of the Bible and found himself rereading parts of scripture. His new neighbor asked about Sunday school for the kids and Fred told them about how wonderful things were at his church and offered to meet them there. Before he knew it Sunday worship was the highlight and anchor of his week. He was reading his Bible again, praying on a regular basis, and involved in church activities through the week.

"Why then?" Fred asked the empty cross at the front of the church. "I'm back. I'm living faithfully again. Why are things so difficult?"

His eye had never roamed before, yet when the girl behind the counter at his coffee shop flirted with him one morning his heart started racing. When she gave him her number on a napkin he didn't throw it away.

He had never been tempted to cheat at work before but the boss was pressuring him to close files and boost productivity. Fred knew if he just signed off instead of doing the inspections he could probably get the promotion that was coming up.

He reached into his pocket and felt the refund check that had shown up unexpectedly. The kids needed new clothes, the dryer was on its last legs, and the money would go a long way to covering those expenses. Or he could spend the check to buy the new fishing rod he had been trying to save for these past few years.

Fred slumped back in the pew. He closed his eyes and asked the questions that had been tormenting him. "Why am I tempted now like never before? What am I doing wrong?"

When he opened his eyes he noticed that the candles at the front of the church looked like the ones that Linda and he lit when they were married all those years ago. He remembered how nervous he was that day and how much he loved her.

His eye went to the corner behind the choir. He saw the bump in the wall where some repairs had been attempted when he was a boy. When he became a building inspector he knew what had been done wrong and was glad the mistake had been caught otherwise the damage would have been expensive and costly.

The light glinted off the offering plates and he remembered the special appeal made for disaster relief last Sunday to help people who had lost everything. There never seemed to be enough money but his family was well off compared to how some people had to live.

Fred closed his eyes and realized he knew how to deal with the temptation that had been plaguing him. He understood that if he set his mind on God, he would hear again the answers that were both familiar and empowering. Whispering a prayer of thanks Fred got up from the pew more determined than ever to live a life on the way Christ was leading him.

Lent 2
Luke 13:31-35

What You Believe

Simon and Leo sat down with their trays on the other side of the table. They leaned in so Paul could hear them over the din of lunchtime conversations in the cafeteria.

"Paul, can we talk to you?" Simon asked.

Paul looked up from his lunch. "Sure, what's up?"

"We've been hearing things around the school," Simon said. "People are starting to talk about you."

"Good things I hope." Paul took a drink of his soda.

Leo sighed. "I told you he wouldn't take us seriously."

"We have to try. Can you listen to us, Paul?

Paul put down his fork. "Shoot."

"How long have we been friends?"

"The three of us?" Paul thought for a moment. "You and I met in pre-school and Leo moved here the year after."

"So how long has that been?"

Paul did some quick math in his head. "About twelve years. Give or take."

"We have been through thick and thin together, right?"

"Absolutely," Paul said.

"We've been there for each other?"

"Every step of the way."

"Then what are you doing to us?" Simon asked.

Paul looked around at the tables filled with students eating lunch. "Having a meal together?"

"You're ruining things for us," Simon said. "People are talking."

Leo turned to Simon. "Calm down, man."

73

"I can't calm down." Simon raised his voice. "He doesn't even know what he is doing."

Leo grabbed Simon's arm. "You realize people are starting to stare, don't you?"

Simon's face flushed and he lowered his voice. "You talk to him, Leo."

Leo turned to face Paul. "We want you to do something for us."

"Anything."

"We know that you go to church but you know that we don't." Leo gestured at the tables around them. "Neither do most of the other people who go here."

Paul looked around. "I don't actually think that's true."

"Listen, I don't want to argue the point with you," Leo said. "Can you at least agree that talking about God and church isn't a popular thing to do at school?"

"Yeah, so?" Paul sipped at his soda.

"Stop beating around the bush, Leo," Simon muttered. "Get to the point."

"People are starting to say you're one of those religious freaks." Leo took a deep breath. "Because of what you are doing."

"What am I doing?"

"You're organizing one of those Christian student groups here at the school." Simon blurted out. "Why would you do that to us? We're just starting to get accepted by the other kids."

Paul set down his soda. "This is really bothering you, isn't it?"

"You bet," Simon said. Leo nodded.

"Well, I'm sorry. I didn't realize it was a problem for you."

Simon let out a sigh of relief. "Thank goodness. I told you he was reasonable and would listen to us."

Leo narrowed his eyes and considered Paul. "You're not going to stop, are you?"

Paul shook his head.

"Do you want to be an outcast here?" Simon said.

"Not particularly. Jesus is important in my life and if people reject me because I follow him then I guess that is their problem." Paul held up his hand to stop his friends from interrupting. "Yes, it will make me sad and I won't like it but there is no way I can be anything other than the person I am."

"You realize what this will mean to your time here at the school?" Leo asked. "There will be teasing, taunting, and scorning."

"Not to mention going to dances alone," Simon added.

Paul shrugged. "I didn't say I wanted things to be that way but if what is what happens then that's what happens."

"It doesn't have to be that way, all you have to do is stop talking about Jesus." Simon waved his hands. "Don't be part of that group. Then everything will be fine."

Paul shook his head. "No, it wouldn't. It would be worse."

"What can be worse than losing your friends and being alone?"

Paul looked his friend in the eye. "Denying God."

"No one is telling you to deny God." Simon said.

"How is me not being true to God and keeping my mouth shut and not being with other believers not denying God?" Paul asked.

Simon sighed loudly. "We're not asking you to stop believing or going to church. Just don't do any of that stuff here at school."

"All of that stuff is who I am."

"You realize that you might lose the friends you have because of what you are doing?"

Paul looked at his dearest and oldest friends. "I do."

Simon threw up his hands. "You're impossible."
"No," Paul said. "I'm a disciple of Jesus."

Lent 3
Luke 13:1-9

Following the Way

There once was a young man who walked in his life with God. His journey led him to the base of a mountain which had many different paths leading toward the top. At the start of the paths there were people milling about.

"Which way should I go in order to find God?" the young man asked.

"We don't know." The people looked from one path to another. "Just pick one. They all look pretty much the same."

The young man stopped and carefully examined what he could see of the different paths. He noticed a few ended at a large boulder or a fallen tree. "Those don't look like they are the right ways to go."

"Are you sure?" the people asked. "Have you traveled those routes and know there isn't something behind the obstacles?"

The young man took the time to look at the paths carefully from different perspectives. "I don't see anything but a dead end following those ways."

"So how do we know they all aren't dead ends?" The people wrung their hands. "We wish there was a sign."

The young man turned his attention to the paths which headed up the mountain and disappeared from sight. They all looked like they required persistence and perseverance to climb. As he studied them he noticed that on one of them just before the path went out of sight there was a sign which said in bold letters "the way."

"Isn't that a sign?" he said.

The people shrugged. "Other travelers have thought so but we don't know if we can trust that sign. We're waiting for something more definite."

The young man considered everything he knew and started up the path marked "the way."

"Where are you going?" the people asked.

"Up the mountain to continue on my journey of faith."

"How do you know that is the way you are supposed to travel?" they said.

He pointed. "There is a sign."

"Can you prove the sign is trustworthy?" They wanted to know.

"All I can do is have faith." The young man extended his hand. "Do any of you want to come with me?"

No one would go with him. The young man climbed the path and as he went around the bend the people behind him disappeared from sight.

He continued walking and saw that the way split into two directions. One was a wide path that had a gentle slope as it continued up the mountain while the other was narrow and rocky and looked like it would take some effort to climb. The narrow path had a signpost which said "the way."

A woman was starting down the wide path.

"Why are you going in that direction?" he called after her. "The sign is on the steep path."

She shook her head. "This way looks easier."

He frowned. "Did the signs lead you on the wrong path before?"

She put her hands on her hips. "Are you telling me that I won't get to the top if I go this way?"

He shook his head. "I don't know where that path leads. Maybe there are many ways to reach God and maybe that path will take you to the top. All I know is that the sign showing the way has not led me astray before."

"I want an easier journey so I'm going down this path." She started down the wide trail.

The young man watched her go out of sight and started up the steep way. He struggled to keep his footing and wondered if he had made a mistake when he looked back and saw how far he had come. He arrived at another fork in the path and saw a man standing at the crossroads.

The young man pointed at one of the paths. "The sign says that God is that way."

"I think I am finished my journey of faith." The man sat down. "I've been good and virtuous. I have done everything that was expected of me."

"Are you sure you're done traveling?" The young man looked around the small clearing. "This doesn't look like our destination. I can help you if you need someone to give you a hand."

The man shook his head. "I am perfectly capable of making my own way thanks. There is nothing wrong with my feet or legs. I am just not going any further."

"Why not?" the young man asked. "I think we are close to our destination."

"It doesn't matter," the man said. "I am not doing anything more."

The young man shook his head and continued up the path marked clearly with the sign. It wasn't far when he reached the top of the mountain and realized that his journey was over.

Looking back he could see the way he had come and realized that even though the climb had not always been easy it had always been in his grasp because his way to God was clearly marked.

Lent 4
Luke 15:1-3, 11b-32

Answering with Grace

"What is Tina doing home?" Silvia asked. "The last I heard she sold her share of the family business and swore to never come back again."

"That was a while ago." Hazel picked out a large turkey and placed it in her shopping cart. "She went to the city for a while."

"If she is back then I bet she ran out of money." Silvia looked over the selection in the display case and turned up her nose.

"Yes, she did." Hazel pointed to the shelf. "Can you hand me some cranberry?"

Silvia grabbed a can and handed it to Hazel. "I bet she spent her inheritance on booze and gambling."

"I never asked."

Silvia snorted. "You mean she never told you."

"No, I mean I really don't care." Hazel looked at her cart and did some calculations. "Could you hand me one more?"

"How could you not care?" Silvia handed another can to her friend. "It was your money she spent."

"I gave her the inheritance when she asked so it was her money to use as she wanted." Hazel started toward the other end of the store.

Silvia trailed behind her with her own cart. "I would be furious if one of my kids disrespected me and then wasted the money on clubbing with those types of men."

"What makes you think that she did those things?"

"She wasted the money, didn't she?" Silva reached for a bag of discounted candy. "How else do you think she spent it?"

"I told you I didn't ask." Hazel stopped to look at pumpkin pies. "Which ones do you like?"

"Those ones are expensive but they're good." Silvia pointed. "I hoped you put her in her place when she showed up at your door."

"She was gaunt, dressed in dirty work clothes, and looked terrible. She started to apologize and say she wasn't worthy enough to be my daughter." Hazel put three pies in the cart.

"She certainly isn't. Imagine treating your mother like she did. If she was my daughter I would have slammed the door in her face and never let her in," Silvia said. "I suspect you didn't do that."

"Of course I let her in. After all it is her house." Hazel put a bag of potatoes on the bottom of the cart. "I got her some new clothes and got her settled into her old room."

"At least tell me that you paid close attention to her explanation." Silvia grabbed a small box of instant potatoes. "You can throw that up in her face for the rest of her life."

Hazel stopped the cart almost bumping into Silvia. "What are you talking about?"

"Her so-called apology," Silvia said. "As if any words could make things better."

"I have no idea what she said. I was too busy crying and hugging her to listen." Hazel headed toward the produce section and started filling the cart with carrots and squash.

Silvia grabbed some dented cans along the way. "Hazel, you realize she is taking advantage of you."

"Who?"

"Tina, your daughter. The one who wasted her inheritance and came home with hat in hand." Silvia narrowed her eyes. "Do you even know if she is truly sorry for everything that happened?"

"Does it matter?"

"Of course it matters." Silvia picked up some candied yams, looked at them, and then put them back. "You have to be sure that she has really changed and isn't the same selfish girl who broke your heart when she left. You cried for months, as I remember."

"Her leaving was the worst day of my life." Hazel headed for the checkout. "Every day I hoped and prayed that she would come home."

Silvia caught up to her friend. "Hazel, you need to do something to make sure she knows how you feel."

Hazel looked at her cart. "I am doing something."

"What?" Silvia followed Hazel's gaze. "You're shopping at the grocery store."

"Yes, I'm having a huge dinner party to celebrate Tina's return." Hazel pointed at the cart. "Didn't you notice me buying everything?"

Silvia took a step back. "Why in heaven's name would you do such a thing given the way she left you and hurt you?"

"None of that matters."

"Then could you please tell me what does matter and what you are trying to show your wayward daughter by throwing a party for her?"

Hazel looked at her friend and smiled. "I'm showing that I love her and forgive her."

Lent 5
John 12:1-8

Worship and Service

"The money should be used to help the poor." Peter crossed his arms. "We shouldn't be spending it on new carpet for the church."

"I think we are well overdue for some renovations." Stephen knelt down and ran his fingers through the frayed edges where the carpet met the wooden floor. "This is literally falling apart."

Peter shook his head. "It is extravagant and wasteful. This sanctuary is used only an hour a week on Sunday morning."

"It is used for choir practice, the Wednesday evening prayer meeting, Saturday morning hymn sing, and on a number of other occasions through the week." Stephen looked around. "If it were in better shape I think we could do even more."

Peter scowled. "That's not the point. We should be spending the church offering on helping people not on buying things. Jesus said for us to love others as we love ourselves. New carpet doesn't do that."

"Jesus also said that we were to love God with all our heart and soul and strength and mind."

"We do that by loving others."

Stephen rubbed his chin. "So there is no place for worship, prayer, and study?"

"There is place for it, of course." Peter tapped his chest. "All of that happens inside of us. We can worship no matter what the place looks like. There is no justification for spending money in here."

"Except this is where we hold our Sunday worship services and all of those other things that I mentioned." Stephen pointed at the rest of the church. "This building shows others what we believe about God."

"No, it doesn't," Peter said. "This is just the place we gather."

"Then why was it so important for you to have your daughter get married here last summer?"

Peter paused for a moment and then unfolded his arms. "Okay, maybe this isn't just any place and maybe there are lots of great memories and experiences here. I'll even agree that this is a holy place. However, paint and carpet doesn't make it holy — the people who come here do."

"No argument about the people being essential for this being a holy place." Stephen looked at the front door. "What do you think people see when they come through the doors on Sunday?"

Peter shrugged. "They see a church."

"They do. But what do the faded paint, the threadbare carpet, and the shabby surroundings say about the faith of the people in this church?"

"It says that we care more about mission than about buildings."

"Really?" Stephen touched a water stain on the wall of the church. "I think maybe it says that we don't care."

"Why would you say that?"

Stephen pointed toward the faded paint on the ceiling. "If this was either of our homes we would have done repairs a long time ago."

"It's not that bad," Peter said.

"Honestly?" Stephen turned to face his friend. "If this was your house and you had visitors coming how would you feel?"

Peter looked around again and grimaced. "Maybe it could use a little work."

"I think it is long overdue."

"Perhaps the carpet could be replaced."

"I think we need to draw up a list of what needs to be done," Stephen said. "So we have a sanctuary that expresses what we believe about God."

"Wait a second." Peter held up a hand. "Just because I agree there are some things that need to be done doesn't mean that I think mission should take a back seat to renovating this building."

Stephen nodded. "I agree."

"You do?"

"Of course. Honoring God and serving other people are essential to our faith." Stephen pulled out a notepad and started to write. "Personally I think that when we do both things we truly follow Christ."

Peter narrowed his eyes. "So you would have no objection to a gospel concert to raise money for the street mission?"

"I think it would be a great way of inviting people to our church," Stephen said. "I would be happy to help you organize it."

"I would be happy to have your help." Peter reached out his hand. "And I would be willing to help you organize the work here in the church. My son-in-law has some contacts in the construction trades and I think I can get us some good deals."

Stephen took the offered hand and shook it. "That sounds perfect."

The two men then began to work on how to refresh the sanctuary of the church and revitalize a ministry they both believed was essential to their Christian life and witness.

Passion / Palm Sunday
Luke 19:28-40

Seeds of Faith

There once was a woman who followed Jesus with all her heart. She prayed regularly, read her Bible constantly, and allowed the Spirit to guide her life. She felt called to travel and live in a city far away from home. She met the neighbors in this new place and since she was a kind person made friends quickly. The neighbors in this new city appreciated the woman and the way she lived but there were a few things they didn't understand.

"What are you doing?" they asked when she bowed her head before eating.

"I'm praying."

"What is praying?" they wanted to know.

"Praying is when we talk to God."

"Who is God?"

"God is the one who created everything and God loves us very much," the woman explained. "I pray to tell God about my day and to thank God for all the wonderful things I have been blessed with."

The neighbors had never heard about God and were excited that the one who created the universe loved them and was interested in them. Even those who were not sure about whether there was a God didn't mind people praying. They could appreciate being thankful and considered it a virtue to be grateful for the good things of life. The neighbors were excited to learn about prayer and wanted to know how the woman knew about these things. The woman showed them her Bible.

"What is that?" they asked as she opened the pages.

"This is a Bible."

"Does it tell about prayer?" they wanted to know.

"It has prayers in it," she explained. "Yet there is much more to the Bible. The Bible is a book that tells us about God's love for all people and about Jesus."

The neighbors were very interested and eagerly listened as she read them the parables of Jesus and some stories of his life from the gospels.

"Jesus sounds like a wonderful man. Where are the places you are talking about and when did all of this take place?"

"Jesus lived a long time ago in another land," she explained. "He came to show us God in his life and through his words."

The neighbors thought that was very fine and each day on the bus eagerly listened to the Bible as she read them some of the stories of Jesus. There were great discussions and debates about what Jesus taught and the miracles that he performed. Even the people who didn't know whether they believed that Jesus did the wondrous things the Bible described had to admit that being kind to people and caring about those in need were good things to encourage.

All in all people were quite eager and pleased that the woman had moved to their city, taught them about prayer, and shared the stories of Jesus. That was until one day when someone asked how Jesus died.

"He was crucified and buried," the woman explained.

"That's horrible," the neighbors said. "Why would anyone want to hurt Jesus?"

"He pointed out how those in power were being hypocrites because they were not doing the good things that God wants in the world," the woman explained. "Jesus taught that God cannot be denied and should be the ruler in our hearts."

This confused the people. "Jesus died like a criminal. He must have been wrong."

The woman shook her head. "On the third day Jesus rose from the dead and God has made him the King of kings and Lord of lords. He came to save not just the people long ago or in places far away but all people in all places. His death and resurrection happened so that we can live new lives right now."

The neighbors talked about her words among themselves. Some were quite upset by what the woman said. "You can't say that!"

"Why not?"

"Because there are people who will be upset by it and things in our land might change if people know about Jesus. You need to stop praying and teaching," those neighbors declared. "You are upsetting the way things are."

"You heard about prayer and thought it was a good thing," the woman said. "You heard about Jesus and thought he had great things to say."

"We did, but now we need you to stop before things change in ways we can't control."

"Hasn't that already happened because you know about God and Jesus?" she asked.

The neighbors talked about her words with a great deal of discussion and debate. Many felt that any and all steps needed to be taken to stop people from knowing about Jesus because if things changed they might get worse. A few, though, had taken to heart all that the woman said and began to hope that because of Jesus their world would continue to change for the better.

Maundy Thursday
John 13:1-17, 31b-35

Priorities in Life

"Jake is so dreamy." Melissa sat her drink on the table and sighed.

Susan looked up from her magazine. "I guess if you like that type."

"You mean the tall, dark, and handsome type of man?"

Susan shrugged. "I guess he is good looking."

"I mean he has everything." Melissa looked down the corridor where Jake and his friends sat laughing. "He has a chiseled jaw, great hair, and a smile that makes my heart pitter-patter."

Susan rolled her eyes. "You're almost eighty, Melissa. Act your age."

"Why?" Melissa giggled. "I mean you have to admit he is a catch."

"He's good to look at but beyond that?" Susan shook her head. "I want something different in a man."

"You're looking?" Melissa's eyes went wide. "I thought that you were going to stay single."

Susan closed her magazine. "Sometimes it is nice to have a man around, you know. Someone to help out around the house."

"You do remember that we are living in a senior's complex where everything is done for us, don't you?"

"Of course I do. I don't mean mowing the lawn or fixing the sink." Susan fiddled with her hands as she thought. "I just want someone around to talk to and who knows me better than anyone else. You know what I mean."

"Tom and I used to talk for hours after he retired." Melissa's eyes misted over. "He was a good man."

"I know." Susan patted her friend's hand. "I miss Fred and it has been almost thirty years."

The two women sat in silence for a few minutes. Melissa snuck a glance at Susan.

"So have you ever thought about it?"

"About what?"

"Getting married again." Melissa looked down the corridor where Jake and some of the other men from the senior's home were playing dominoes. "Sometimes I think about it."

"With Jake?"

"Jake is fine, don't get me wrong, and to make my children and friends blush and get all flustered I might mention his name." She poked Susan in the side. "But if I am going to take the plunge again I am looking for something more."

"Like what?"

"I want someone like Jesus."

Susan examined her friend's face. "You're serious."

"I am. I want a good Christian man."

"Well, there are lots of them in church each Sunday."

"There are a lot of men in church on Sunday because we're getting older and each time one of us gets sick or dies the others are reminded that we're not here forever," Melissa said. "What I want is a man who really loves God and lives out that love."

"It would be nice to have a godly man in my life. I loved Fred for sure but when it came to faith he really didn't have much time." Susan narrowed her eyes. "You have someone in mind, don't you?"

Melissa's face went scarlet.

Susan moved closer to her friend. "Who is it?"

Melissa's voice dropped to a whisper. "Gordon."

"Gordon?" Susan tapped her fingers on the chair as she thought. "He moved in last month, didn't he?"

Melissa nodded. "I never paid him much attention until I saw him with his granddaughter."

"The little girl who has Down's syndrome and the cutest smile ever?"

"That's the one."

"When we went out to the bus he was playing cards with her."

"That's nice." Susan tilted her head to one side. "What's so special about that?"

"When we came back four hours later they were still playing cards." Melissa looked over at the table near the door. "He was so patient and gentle with her. She spilled her drink a couple of times and he never raised his voice. One time she cried and he just held her and reminded her that everyone spills things on occasion."

Susan sat up. "Really?"

Melissa nodded. "Then he went over to the piano and played for her while she sang. That was when his face lit up."

"She's a good singer?"

"Not really," Melissa said. "He sang all of the old gospel favorites with her. When they finished he hugged her and told her she was a gift from God."

"And from that you want to marry him?"

"Of course not, I haven't gone senile." Melissa snapped. She looked over to where Gordon's room was. "I like what I've seen so far and honestly having a good Christian friend is worth more than anything else, isn't it?"

"I agree." Susan pulled out a compact and fixed her hair. "Maybe I should get to know him too."

"I think we both should." Melissa glared at her friend. "Remember, though, if he's the marrying kind I saw him first."

The two women locked eyes. After a moment they burst out laughing and started toward Gordon's room to welcome him to the complex and to get to know another disciple of Jesus.

Good Friday
John 18:1—19:42

Hearing the Good News

There was a small congregation in church on Good Friday. The large crowds that waved their palms and shouted hosanna the Sunday before had given way to a collection of lost souls who gathered in the darkened sanctuary to listen to the passion narrative.

John was there because his wife dragged him to the service. He wasn't a great fan of church but came with her because she asked him repeatedly. It wasn't that he had any great objection to God, or the Bible, or what happened in worship. It was just that he didn't find it had much to do with him. As the service began his mind started to wander. He was daydreaming about the movie he was going to watch when they got home. He hoped the kids hadn't found his stash of chips in the garage. He wondered if he would be able to spend some time on Monday working on his latest pet project.

"Who are you looking for?"

The words echoed around John and his mind snapped to attention. He realized that one of the reasons he agreed to come with Cheryl was that he was hoping for more in his life. He wanted to know God and God's presence. For the first time in a long time, John actually listened to the words of scripture being read.

Cheryl looked over at John sitting attentively. She wondered what had gotten into him. She knew that he didn't like church because of the way he dragged himself on the mornings they came. Honestly after ten years of marriage she wondered if she had made the wrong choice. She was angry with him more often than not. He never seemed to think about anything but himself. He didn't appreciate her the way he should. He didn't deserve her and all that she did for him.

"Put your sword away."

The words echoed around Cheryl and she flushed. Her hand crept over and tentatively took John's. He looked over and squeezed her hand and in that moment she knew he loved her. She wiped the corner of her eye and focused her attention on the service.

Paulette started to wonder if she had made a mistake that morning. Her eyes took in the man and woman holding hands as they listened to the scriptures being read. She had come to church because she was lonely and her life was in shambles. She needed to know that she wasn't alone. She desperately wanted to feel that someone cared. She wished she could find something in this church service to let her know that she was loved. Could Jesus really love someone as pitiful as her?

"Do you ask this on your own, or did others tell you about me?"

The words echoed around Paulette and she found herself remembering her grandmother taking her to church, telling her the stories of Jesus, and teaching her how to pray. She knew at that moment she wanted to believe again and needed to know grace once more. She longed to recapture the feeling of peace she knew when her grandmother was alive. She opened her heart and found herself starting to hope that Jesus did care about her. She dared to believe that he had gone to the cross because she was important to him.

Pastor Greg looked out at the small number of people listening to the story of the passion being read. He knew that in a few days the church would be filled with people coming to hear the Easter story and wished with all of his heart that more people would come out to hear of Jesus' crucifixion. He believed in the life changing power of the gospel and it hurt him to see so few people coming out to this service.

He wanted people to know Jesus and he prayed as the scriptures were read that in some way the Holy Spirit would work through the words. That somehow even these few people would find something, anything that would help anchor their faith and let them know the richness and bounty of God's great love.

"It is finished."

The words echoed around Pastor Greg and he took in the scattered faces of the congregation. Some of them were thoughtful, some of them were crying, some of them almost shone with peace. He closed his eyes and offered a prayer of thanks for the words of the gospel and the difference that the story of the cross makes in the lives of those who hear it proclaimed.

Easter Sunday
John 20:1-18

New Beginnings

Tammy tossed and turned. She fluffed her pillow, rolled over, and tried to go back to sleep. Yet when she closed her eyes she relived every moment of the argument. She heard Jared's words again and again — *You're a terrible mother. I hate you. I wish Dad hadn't died.* She saw the hatred and pain in his face. Tears flowed down her cheeks. It was all too much. She was barely getting through each day as it was. Kevin had been their rock and without him they were spiraling out of control.

She wiped her face. She knew she made the right choice telling Jared he couldn't go out. The more he told her about where he was going and who he would be with the more she grew suspicious and uneasy. As his story fell apart under her questions, he became more and more belligerent and soon the shouting and accusations started. Finally she realized there was no other choice but to order him to his room and the slammed door was the last she heard or saw from him.

The clock said it was still well before five in the morning. She closed her eyes and after a few moments realized there was no way she was going back to sleep. She threw off the sheets and put on her robe. She paused next to Jared's room but everything was quiet. She made her way down to the kitchen and put on a pot of coffee. She picked up the church service bulletin from Good Friday and noticed the time for the sunrise service being held at the top of the lookout. She sighed. Someday maybe she would be able to go.

Quite honestly though right now she was too upset, too shaken by what had happened to even think about church.

She poured herself a cup of coffee and grabbed one of the hot cross buns she had baked earlier in the week. She sipped, ate, and tried to calm down. She was just starting to relax when she heard Jared's door creak. Her hands gripped her mug and her heart raced. He was trying to sneak out. How dare he defy her in that way? She steeled herself to confront him when footsteps sounded on the stairs.

"Where do you think you are going?" she demanded as soon as he came into view. "Why are you carrying your baseball bat?"

"I heard a noise in the kitchen and came to investigate." He started to retreat up the stairs. "I didn't know you were up. I'll leave you alone."

Tammy's righteous anger evaporated as she realized he was wearing his pajamas and slippers. She took a deep breath. She shouldn't have leapt to conclusions. She shouldn't have snapped.

"Do you want a hot cross bun?" She pushed the plate toward him.

Jared slunk down the stairs, set his bat up against the wall and slumped into a chair.

"Can I have some coffee to go with it?"

"In five years maybe." She poured him a glass of milk.

He scowled. "I bet dad would have let me drink coffee."

Tammy laughed. There were some things that she and Kevin had always agreed on. "I seriously doubt that, don't you?"

Jared shrugged and took the offered milk. They ate and drank in silence for a few moments.

"Sorry about last night," Jared muttered. "I kind of lost it. I just wanted to go out with my friends. Can we let it go?"

"We're going to have to talk about last night at some point." Tammy cleared her throat. "But neither of us are up for that right now, are we?"

Jared gave a reluctant nod and continued eating. He finished his milk and pushed back from the table. "Can I go back to bed?"

Tammy nodded.

Jared paused at the bottom of the stairs. "You staying up?"

She glanced down at the service bulletin. "You know, I think I might go to the sunrise service up at the lookout."

"Can I come?"

She looked at her son in amazement. "You want to go to church?"

"Yeah," he said. "It's outside and sounds neat."

"It does sound interesting, doesn't it?" Tammy smiled. "Can you be ready in ten minutes?"

"Can I wear jeans and a T-shirt?"

"It's outside — I can't imagine why not."

"Be back in five." Jared dashed up the stairs.

Tammy watched him go and began to smile. Maybe this would be the day when things would change for the better. Maybe the darkness would give way to the dawn. Maybe there was a new life that was possible for them after death. She headed up the stairs and began to smile as hope took root in her heart and began to grow.

Easter 2
John 20:19-31

Answering Doubt

Sally sat at the bus stop staring at the 'Happy Easter' sign in front of the church. She sighed. She wished she could believe.

"Is something the matter?"

Sally blushed when she noticed an old woman sitting next to her. "Sorry, I thought I was alone."

The old woman looked from side to side. "No, just us here."

Sally waved her hand. "It's nothing important."

"Such a sigh like that is always important." The old woman tilted her head to one side. "Maybe though you do not like to talk about these things to strangers. So I will tell you I am Mary."

Sally smiled. "I'm Sally."

"Good." Mary clapped her hands together. "Now we are not strangers but are becoming friends. So tell me, Sally my new friend, what is it that made you sigh so deeply?"

"Just thinking about things."

"Ahh, you were deep in thought," Mary said. "What is it that makes you sigh as if your heart was breaking?"

Sally pointed at the church across the street. "I was just looking over there."

"It is not a church I have ever been in. Is it a good church?"

"I think so. I used to go there."

"You do not go there anymore." Mary rubbed her chin. "So is there another church that you go to?"

"No," Sally said. "I have not been to any church in a long time."

Mary nodded. "Sally my new friend, I think I would sigh very deeply if I did not have my church or another church to go to. Do you know why?"

Sally looked over at the old woman. "Why?"

"In the country where I grew up in there were many people who did not like those of us who follow Jesus." She pulled up her sleeve to show a small cross tattoo on her wrist. "I had to get this when I was a girl younger than you because if I did not then some of the men might take me to be their wife and beat me if I tried to go to church or pray to Jesus."

"Really?"

"Yes, it is hard in my homeland for those of us who believe in Jesus."

"Is that why you came here to live?"

"They came for us who were Christians in the night and we had to run for our lives." Mary's eyes grew hard. "It was a very difficult time."

"That's terrible."

"Yes. I am one of the lucky ones to make it here where I can go to my church and pray and sing without worrying about men with guns or police coming to arrest us." Mary looked away at the distance and then patted Sally's hand. "But we are not talking about my troubles. God is good and now I am more blessed than ever. I have a new friend. So tell me Sally why are you sighing looking at your old church. Have you been told to never come back?"

Sally shook her head. "No, I'm sure the pastor and everyone else would welcome me back with open arms. They would be happy to see me."

Mary cocked her head to one side. "Then why do you not go through the doors?"

Sally's voice dropped to a whisper. "I'm not sure I believe any more."

"Ah child, I am so sorry for you." Mary's eyes filled with tears. "It must be hard to remember the joy of being part of the church and now standing separate. Can your new friend Mary tell you something?"

"Sure."

"Jesus still loves you even when you have doubts and he will meet you where you are." Mary's smile burst forth in her face. "I learned that when I was afraid and wondered why the bad things were happening to me and my family."

"I wish I could believe that," Sally said.

A bus pulled up at the stop and Mary stood up.

"I will believe it for you if you find it too hard right now." Mary leaned over and kissed Sally on the forehead. "And I will pray for you my new friend that your eyes will see Jesus or his angel inviting you to come back to his people."

Sally watched as the old woman climbed onto the bus. She wondered if she would ever find answers to her doubts. As the bus pulled away Mary appeared in the window and waved. The cross tattooed on the old woman's wrist caught her eye and something changed within Sally.

After the bus was gone from sight Sally got off the seat, crossed the road, and headed toward the church of her childhood. She still had many questions but one thing she knew for certain. Sally had been invited that day to return to her faith not because she no longer had doubts but because those doubts did not stop God from being part of her life.

Easter 3
John 21:1-19

Faithful Bounty

George took a sand bag and put it on top of the pile. He reached for another and realized that there were no more in the stack. He looked over and saw Jennifer heading his way with a wheel barrow filled with more bags and took the opportunity to stretch his muscles. He stepped on one of the bags and looked over the top. The sight on the other side made him clench his jaw tightly. He stepped down and took the sandbag off the top of the wheel barrow and added it to the wall.

"How many bags are left?" he asked.

"These are the last." The strain of the night's work was showing in Jennifer's whole body. "Will they be enough?"

George looked at the makeshift walls they had erected around their life's work. He stepped up on a sandbag and offered his wife a hand. She scowled as she looked at the rising waters on the other side.

"Will it be enough, George?"

George wiped his brow, looked up at the dark clouds, and then back at the river. "No."

Jennifer slumped down against the wall. "So this night has been a waste of time and energy."

"Probably."

George looked away from Jennifer as she covered her face and broke down into tears. He closed his eyes and prayed. *Dear Lord, I know I haven't been a good man but please be merciful and help us.* The rain hit his forehead and his eyes snapped open as another downpour began. He reached over and pulled up Jennifer's hood as he adjusted his own. They sat against the wall as the rain pounded down on them. He put his arm around her and pulled her close.

"Let's get in the car and go."

Her eyes were red as she looked up at him. "You want to abandon everything to the water?"

He shrugged. "We're out of sandbags. The water is still rising. We've failed."

Her eyes closed for a moment and he could see her lips moving. He was going to tell her not to bother praying but who knows, maybe God would listen to her. She had always been a good woman, better than he deserved and had gone to church a lot more than he ever had. George looked over at the house and farm they were trying to save. A lifetime of work was going to be washed away.

"We should go," he said.

Her eyes opened with new determination. "Let's keep working at it."

"Why bother? A few extra bags won't make any difference."

Her hand pointed toward the barn. "George Carver Wainwright, that grain and those animals are earmarked for disaster relief overseas. There are people waiting to get that food and feed the hungry. I'm not giving up when there is something left for us to try."

He threw up his hands "Jennifer, we're done. It would take a miracle for them to be saved."

"Then let's make a miracle happen."

George looked up at the sky. "There is nothing we can do about the rain and the water."

"Then let's do what we can do." Jennifer grabbed the sand bag in the wheel barrow and strained to lift it onto the wall. George shook his head but his hands went to help her. In a few moments they had lifted the last bags into place.

"Well, that's all we can do."

Jennifer grabbed a shovel. "What about a ditch to divert any that comes over the wall?"

"It won't be enough."

"Will it hurt?"

He rubbed his chin for a moment. He walked to where the wall was the weakest and began to outline a ditch with the heel of his boot. Jennifer started to dig and George grabbed another shovel and dug with her. Before long there was water flowing over the wall and down through the ditch.

"Will it be enough?" Jennifer asked.

George narrowed his eyes and looked at what they had done. "If the forecasts are correct and the flood crests by morning we might be able to keep the water from being more than a few feet. We're probably going to lose the grain."

Jennifer glared at the barn. "How do we save it?"

"Woman, you just don't give up, do you?"

She turned to him with fire burning in her eyes. "Man, why would I give up when God gave me the ability to keep going?"

"Even if we do everything we can we might still fail."

Her head shook with energy and certainty. "God doesn't call us to defeat but to faithfulness."

He took in her determination and felt the fatigue of the night start to slip away. His muscles ached but his mind started to think again. "We could put it on pallets. That might work."

Jennifer started toward the barn. George let a smile cross his lips and closed his eyes for a moment. *Lord, she is more than I deserve. Thank you for Jennifer and help us to get through this night.*

"Man, are you coming or not?"

George opened his eyes to see his wife glaring at him. "Woman, I was just praying."

Her glare softened. "All right then. Let's go and find out how God is going to answer us."

Easter 4
John 10:22-30

Knowing His Voice

Leah put her cards on the table. "Scott, how do you know when it's Jesus talking to you?"

"Not the conversation I expected when I suggested cards," Scott said. "You just know, I guess."

Leah turned her attention to the players sitting on her left and right. "Is that your experience as well?"

Vera nodded while sorting her cards.

Tom put his down and looked thoughtful. "I find when I pray I hear him speaking to me."

"You mean speaking clearly like we are right now?"

"No, not like that." Tom took a drink from his water and cleared his throat. "I guess the more I pray and walk with Jesus the more I am used to his presence be it speaking through someone else, an event, or even music."

"Occasionally it is something that just comes to me," Vera added. "One moment I am listening and the next I have the answer."

"How are you certain?" Leah asked.

"You know," Vera said. Scott and Tom nodded in agreement.

Leah thought about it for a moment and then picked up her cards and the game continued. They went around the table until every card had been played. Scott added up the score.

"Well I guess that game also goes to you. Play another?"

Tom looked at his watch. "Not for us I'm afraid. Thanks for the delightful evening."

Vera echoed his comments as they said their goodbyes and headed home.

Scott helped Leah clear the table. "That was fun. We should ask them over next Friday night."

"I agree," Leah said. "Their dog wasn't a bother either. She just curled up and was quiet as a church mouse."

Scott looked over at the corner. "Uh. I think she is still here."

"Poor thing is sound asleep." Leah went over and touched the dog gently. The dog's eyes snapped open. "Time for you to go home."

The dog sat up, yawned, stretched, and then laid down again.

"Let me try." Scott went over to the door and opened it. "Your master and mistress have gone home. You should go too."

Nothing happened. Scott and Leah tried encouraging, getting out a treat, and pleading but the dog would not move. Scott leaned down to pick the dog up but she started to growl.

Leah looked at the unmoving dog. "What are we going to do?"

Scott picked up the phone. "I guess they will have to come back and get her. It's not that far of a walk."

Tom picked up on the first ring.

"Your dog is still here," Scott explained.

"I guess she isn't much of a watch dog. is she?" Tom laughed. "Just tell her to go home and open the door. She knows the way and will go through the backyard. She's good like that."

Scott looked over at the stubborn dog. "We tried telling her, opening the door, and pretty much everything we could think of but she hasn't moved."

"Huh. Usually she is a good listener when I tell her to do something."

"I think you might have to come back and get her because both Leah and I have tried but neither of us have had any luck, Tom." Scott watched the dog's ears perk up. "I know she is listening but she isn't doing anything."

"Okay, we'll come back and get her. What's that Vera?" There was some conversation at the other end Scott couldn't make out and then Tom returned. "Can I speak to Leah?"

"Sure." Scott handed the phone over.

"I'm not sure there is anything I can say to add to what Scott told you," Leah said. "The dog isn't paying any attention to us."

"I know but our discussion before we left got me to thinking. I know this sounds strange but put the phone next to the dog."

Leah's eyebrows went up. "You want to talk to the dog?"

"Humor me."

Leah looked over at Scott who shrugged. She knelt down beside the dog. "Okay Tom, go ahead I've put you on speaker."

"Princess, come home," Tom said.

The dog got up, trotted over to the door, and whined. Scott rushed over to open it and the dog disappeared into the night.

"For heaven's sake," Leah said. "She listened to you and she's on her way home."

"That's because she knows my voice," Tom said. "I talk to her all the time and she knows she can trust me and that I care for her. So when I spoke she listened."

Leah hung up and shook her head. "Scott, I never thought I would understand something about my faith because of a dog."

Scott laughed. "God works in mysterious ways."

Easter 5
John 13:31-35

As I Have Loved You

Charley sat up in his hospital bed. "What do you want?"

"I want to visit." Shirley stood in the doorway. "Is that okay?"

Charley laid back down. "Whatever."

"How are you?" Shirley moved a chair beside his bed.

Charley scowled. "How does it look like I'm doing?"

Shirley examined the machines surrounding his bed and looked at all the tubes running into his arms. She couldn't help but notice how gaunt his body and face had become. "You look awful and are probably sick and exhausted from the treatments."

Charley barked out a laugh. "That's the first honest thing anyone has said to me. The nurses tell me that something isn't going to hurt but it does. They tell me the pain killers will take away my nausea and discomfort but they don't. My family tell me I am going to be fine but I just get sicker."

"You look terrible. Telling you something different won't change that fact."

"Exactly." Charley's eyes narrowed. "What are you doing here?"

"You have got no family in town and you have alienated all the neighbors with your sharp tongue."

Charley snorted. "Wow, you don't pull any punches."

"Do you want me to lie to you or to be honest?"

"I know it's true." He turned his head away from her to wipe his eyes. "So are you here because you heard I was dying and think you should save my soul?"

"Nothing would make me happier than having you come to Christ. I know Marjorie always wanted you to go to church." Shirley waited until Charley nodded. "Truthfully though I am just here because I thought you might need someone to talk to."

"Just because you were best friends with my late wife doesn't mean you're my friend."

Shirley stood up. "If you want me to go just say so."

Charley stared at her for a few moments. "I don't want you to preach to me."

"Does this mean that you want me to stay and visit?"

"I don't mind if you sit for a while."

Shirley sat back down. "Have you heard from the kids?"

Charley leaned his head toward the two cards on the ledge. "They call every week out of obligation."

"At least they keep in contact."

"I suppose." Charley reached over and opened one of the cards. "I wish they would come and see me."

"Have you told them that?"

"They should want to be here." Charley put the card back on the window ledge. "I shouldn't have to ask."

"You were a terrible father and got worse after Marjorie died. Why would they want to spend time with you?"

Charley slumped back in his bed. "I know I've made some mistakes with them."

"Tell them that and maybe they'll come to see you."

"It's too late."

Shirley shook her head. "It is never too late."

"Marjorie always used to say that." Charley gave her a weak smile. "I'll think about it."

Shirley took a deep breath. "So how bad is it?"

Charley looked up at the ceiling. "Really bad."

"I'm sorry." She reached over and took his hand. He grasped it and squeezed for a moment before letting go. "Is there anything I can do?"

"Turn back time so I can live a better life and not mess up my marriage and my family?" Charley said. "Nothing else really matters to me right now."

"You can't undo the past but you can do something about it." Shirley pointed at the cards. "They haven't cut you off completely. Call them and apologize. Tell them you're sorry."

"You honestly think that will make things any better?"

"It's certainly better than sitting here doing nothing but regretting the past."

"Maybe I'll call them after supper. With the time difference, Tim should be home from work. After that I could call Rita." Charley started to cough and pressed the pain pump strapped to his bed.

Shirley got up from her chair. "I think you need to rest."

Charley reached out and grabbed her hand. "Can you do something for me before you go?"

"What?"

"Can you pray for me?"

"I could but there is something better that I can do for you."

"What's that?"

"I can pray with you."

Charley sighed. "I can't imagine Jesus listening to a terrible sinner like me."

"I can't imagine Jesus not listening to a terrible sinner like you."

Charley frowned at her for a moment and then burst out laughing. Shirley sat down in the chair and waited for him to stop.

"Okay," he said. "I'll pray with you. Because if a good Christian like you can spend time with me then I guess I have to believe that Jesus would as well."

They bowed their heads and together prayed for forgiveness, strength, and peace for both Charley and his family.

Easter 6
John 14:23-28

Finding Peace

David paced around the room. His groomsmen sat in the corner texting and surfing on their phones. They invited him to have a seat and laughed when he shook his head and kept moving. Finally he stepped into the hallway and walked to the window to look at the cars in the parking lot. He examined the bulletin board for a moment and then perched on the bench in the hallway. His fingers tapped on the arm rest and he shifted in his seat.

"You okay, son?"

David turned around to see Abe, the caretaker, standing there with a broom in one hand and a dustpan in the other. "Yeah, I'm fine or at least I will be."

Abe narrowed his eyes. "No one is forcing you to get married, are they?"

David shook his head. "Just nervous, I guess."

"I have seen lots of people waiting to be married and I know what jitters look like."

Abe set the broom and dustpan against the wall. "Something tells me you have more on your mind."

"I should be in better shape," David said. "Everyone says this is the happiest day of my life."

Abe shrugged his shoulders. "You can be anxious and happy at the same time."

David's voice quivered. "I'm scared."

"Every man who ever lived was scared heading to the altar." Abe rubbed his chin. "Since you stood with most of your groomsmen when they got married you know that to be a fact. So what's the real problem?"

David sat in silence for a few moments. "I'm worried."

"About what in particular?"

"Nothing. Everything." David's face scrunched up. "My mind just races and I can't stop thinking about all the bad things that might happen."

"And?"

David's eyes widened. "Isn't that enough?"

"Sure but I imagine you've had times in your life like that before. I saw you at the Christmas pageant as a young boy when you were so anxious you almost threw up on the stage. I watched as you mooned over Valerie in youth groups before you two finally got together. You love her and she is crazy for you. What's the real problem?"

David took a deep breath. "I've tried everything. I've taken quiet walks, practiced meditation, listened to calming music, even picked up some candles that were supposed to help me relax. I can't find it."

Abe's brow went up. "Find what?"

"Peace." David sighed. "I want to be as good a man for Valerie as Pops was to Mom. I believe in Jesus and I have faith that what we are doing is the right thing. Why can't I find peace in my life?"

"Your father was a good man and if he was here he would certainly tell you. Since he's not I'd be pleased to offer you my help." Abe patted David on the shoulder. "That's actually a simple one for me to answer."

David turned to face the older man. "Really?"

"Sure." Abe looked his young friend in the eye. "You have been thinking of peace as something you do, the result of knowing the right words or moving in the proper way."

"Absolutely." David nodded. "Am I doing something wrong?"

"Kind of." Abe's eyes flicked over to the stack of wrapped boxes near the door. "What did you do to deserve those?"

"David's eyes followed his gaze. "Nothing. They are wedding presents."

"Yet you and Valerie get to enjoy them, don't you?"

David nodded.

"Jesus told the disciples that peace was a gift."

David's brow furrowed. "So how do I get peace in my life?"

"Like you get any gift. Open your hands to receive it." Abe smiled. "You have faith in Jesus and you trust in God? If so then give God your burdens and let God give you peace."

"That sounds too simple."

Abe snorted. "Some things are simple. When God is involved most of what we need to do is simply accept and believe."

"So if I tell God that I am nervous then my fear and worries will go away?"

"That's up to you. If you let your faith and hope be greater and if you ask for peace then your worries and fears might still be there but they won't be important." Abe's eyes twinkled. "God has a way of putting things into perspective for us."

David bowed his head for a moment before opening his eyes. "I think I'm ready."

"Good." Abe pointed down the hall. "The pastor is looking for you."

David jumped up to his feet. "How do I look?"

Abe's face broke into a wide grin. "You look like a man who is marrying the love of his life and looking forward to it."

Ascension of Our Lord
Luke 24:44-53

Witness to These Things

"I don't understand." Alice stared at the rejection letter in her hands. "Aren't I qualified?"

"You have all the academic qualifications we could ask for in a youth minister," Tabitha said. "In fact the whole committee was impressed by your grasp of Greek and Hebrew and the traveling you've done in the Holy Land."

"I thought my experiences would be an asset in working with young people." Alice frowned.

"Everyone on the hiring committee could tell you are passionate about biblical history and relating that to modern life."

"Yet you still said *no* to me." Alice looked at Tabitha. "Did I do something wrong in the interview?"

Tabitha shook her head. "You were polished, well spoken, and came across as a very likeable person."

"Then why? Was it my lack of job experience?" Alice thumbed through her papers and pulled out her resume. "I've worked with young people throughout my life."

"You certainly have." Tabitha cleared her throat. "The problem is that you have no experience in the church."

"What do you mean? I've been to seminary." Alice pointed at her academic achievements. "I've given talks about archeology to youth groups and conferences all over the country. How could you say that I have no church experience?"

Tabitha pulled her chair closer to Alice. "This is why I asked the committee to come and speak to you personally. We thought you might not understand why we're going with a different candidate."

"You're right. I don't understand." Alice put her papers down. "I can quote the Bible in the original languages. I've seen all the places described in the gospels and my past experience shows I've proven that I can work with young people."

"No one doubts that at all," Tabitha said.

"Then why are you not hiring me?" Alice held up the letter.

Tabitha looked her squarely in the eye. "Who is Jesus?"

"He was the one called the Messiah by the followers he had in first century Palestine." Alice furrowed her brow. "What does that have to do with anything?"

"Who is Jesus to you?"

Alice swallowed. "He was a great teacher and a good man who lived a long time ago."

Tabitha sat back in her chair. "That's the problem we had with hiring you."

"Why?" Alice closed her eyes. "I can quote the doctrine and creeds of the church. I can recite whole passages of the Bible from memory in the original languages as well as in translation."

"Do you believe it to be true?"

Alice opened her eyes. "What do you mean?"

"Is Jesus the one who shows you the purpose and intention of the scriptures? Do you believe that he came to show you God?"

"Do my personal beliefs matter?" Alice said. "I can teach the youth of the church the material you give and make sure they know it. Don't you want your young people to be informed?"

"We do." Tabitha held up her hand so she could continue. "More importantly we want them to believe it. We want them to come to know Jesus through those things and experience the grace and love God offers us through him."

"How could anyone possibly do that?"

"By telling them your personal story and helping them to believe what you believe," Tabitha said. "That's why Jesus told the disciples when he ascended that they were witnesses to these things."

"They did see those things."

Tabitha nodded. "And so has every believer who has ever walked the earth."

"I don't understand."

"I have felt Jesus in my life. I've known his grace and love. I've felt his mercy and forgiveness." Tabitha smiled. "That makes the stories of Jesus, the message of the Bible something that I can understand because it has happened to me."

Alice sat silently for a few minutes looking at the rejection letter. "I don't think I'm the person to lead your youth ministry."

"I know."

Alice folded up the letter. "I appreciate you taking the time to tell me in person."

"You're very welcome," Tabitha said. "I did however want to say something else."

"What's that?"

"I'd like to tell you how I came to know Jesus in my life," Tabitha said. "I taught physics at the university for many years."

"I didn't know that," Alice said. "What made you believe?"

Tabitha sat back and shared her story of faith.

The Sunday following Alice came with her to church and began to participate in the life of the congregation, not as a youth leader but as one of the people looking to know Jesus in their lives.

Easter 7
John 17:20-26

Together as One

Jack shuffled along the sidewalk beside the church. He paused by an open door and listened to the sounds of happy conversation and laughter. He took a step forward and peered in. People were eating and talking in the hall around tables. He took another step forward and the smell of roast turkey and fresh bread embraced him. His empty stomach rumbled in response. Jack took a step back and bumped into something. He tried to turn but his legs gave out. A pair of strong arms caught him before he fell.

"Thanks," Jack said to the man helping him stay upright. "Sometimes it takes me a minute for my legs to start working again."

"No problem." The man pointed at a chair just inside the door. "You think you can make it that far?"

With some help Jack settled into the seat. His mouth watered when he saw the pie and ice cream making it way around the room on a large cart. The man pulled up a chair and sat next to him.

"Were you headed in to have something to eat?"

"Naw, I was just curious when I heard the noise." Jack's stomach rumbled again. "People seem quite happy."

"They sure are enjoying themselves." The man took in the scene and smiled. "There is nothing like a good dinner to lift your spirits."

"Very true." Jack tested his feet and found them more stable. "I didn't mean to make a fuss. I should be on my way."

"Would you like to come in?" the man asked. "I know there are some extra places and there's plenty of food."

Jack watched the conversation going on around the tables. Then he shook his head. "It wouldn't be right. I'm not from this church."

"Which church do you go to?"

"I grew up going to the small church on the other side of the river," Jack said. "You know the one I mean?"

"The stone church with the tall steeple and clock? Yes, I know it well. That's where Pastor Johns is now, isn't it?"

Jack shrugged his shoulders. "Could be. I haven't been there in a while."

"Ah."

"My momma always took me there when we were young. I loved the singing and seeing everyone in their Sunday best." Jack gazed off in the distance. "I spent many a morning and evening in that church."

"Sounds like some great memories," the man said. "You know they still have a wonderful choir and Pastor Johns is a good preacher."

"That was a long time ago. I'm not sure how welcome I would be. I haven't really been that good a person you know." Jack gestured at his tattered coat and scruffy beard. "Fallen on some hard times too."

"I know you would still be welcome there."

"Maybe." Jack struggled to get up. "Well, I should be getting along. Sorry for the trouble."

The man helped him to his feet. "No problem at all."

Jack took a few tentative steps and then slowly walked to the door. At the threshold he turned around. "Can I ask you something?"

"Sure."

"How do you know that I would still be welcome at my old church? I told you I wasn't a very nice person and have done some terrible things in my life."

"Because Jesus loves you just like he loved you when you were a little boy and the church is a group of his followers who try to show that love to the world." The man smiled again.

"That all sounds good up here." Jack pointed toward his head. "But how do you know that they would still welcome me?"

"Because you are welcome here."

Jack snorted. "I doubt that."

"The offer of the meal still stands."

Jack considered the happy people and the wonderful food being served. "I don't know anybody in there."

"You know me. I haven't eaten so we could sit together."

"I don't know." Jack rubbed his chin. "What would the pastor say about you bringing in a bum like me from the streets?"

"I'm Pastor Luke." The man extended his hand. "I would be happy if you came in to have a meal."

Jack took the offered hand. "I'll come in then but I don't want you preaching at me or nothing."

"The offer was for a meal and there are no strings attached to it," Pastor Luke said.

True to his word Pastor Luke didn't preach at him at at all when they ate. In fact, Jack found that he was the one who did all the talking while Pastor Luke and a few other people who joined them listened.

Much to his surprise, as they sat around the table Jack felt the same feeling, the same love, he had felt when he used to go to First Church as a boy even though there was no singing and people weren't wearing their Sunday best.

Pentecost Day
John 14:8-17 (25-27)

Never Alone

"I'm afraid."

James looked around quickly. He hadn't meant to blurt out his thoughts. Thankfully no one was paying any attention to him in the waiting area of the airport. The closest person had earphones on and the couple not far past were engaged in a deep conversation. James sat back in his seat clutching his ticket and passport.

When the applications to go on a mission trip were circulated in youth group, he assumed it would be another fun activity they'd do together. Then one by one his friends dropped out. Marcus got accepted into university. Carl had to stay home and care for his ailing parents. Juanita was offered the job of a lifetime. Suzy got sick and needed to finish summer school to graduate. James found himself sitting alone on a bench in an airport waiting for his flight.

"God, I'm afraid," he whispered.

It wasn't that he hadn't been enthusiastic. After all, going to a mission and making an important contribution was something that excited him. He dreamed of making a difference and threw himself into the intensive sessions to prepare to live in a new culture and speak a different language. The last few weeks had been a whirlwind of activity and he really didn't have much time to think of anything except getting ready. He rubbed his arm that was still sore from the vaccinations. It wasn't until the church service on Sunday when the congregation prayed for the mission, the pastor gave him a blessing, and his mother started to cry that everything hit him. James was going away from home, away from everything and everyone he knew, for almost six months.

He hadn't slept much since Sunday. He spent his time looking over the maps and images of where he was going and reviewing all the things he was supposed to remember. There was so much involved in going to a different country and so much that was expected of him. The pastor had driven that point home to James as he talked about the great work that he was going to do.

He was just a kid though. How was he supposed to make any difference to a country that had seen so much conflict and to people who lived in such desperate need? It wasn't like he was a doctor who could heal people or a government official who could bring money and resources to a problem. He was simply a young man who had some farming experience. He looked at the papers he had been given saying he was going to help with the agricultural projects the mission was sponsoring. He should have paid more attention when he worked those summers on his grandfather's farm. The flight attendant opened the gate for his plane and James wished he had never agreed to this.

"God, I'm really scared." James closed his eyes. "I need your help."

He waited for a sense of peace, or purpose, or something to take away his fear and uncertainty. His flight was announced over the loud speaker and James felt his stomach tie up in knots. He gathered up his bags and got in line to show his boarding pass and passport.

A young woman carrying a knapsack over her shoulder smiled at him. "Are you going to the homeland?"

"Pardon?"

"I could not help but notice the papers you are holding. They mention the hill country in my country."

James glanced at his study material. "I'm working with the mission there."

"They do wonderful things." Her smiled widened. "My uncle's small farm is in the area and a worker from that mission helped him set up better irrigation."

James looked down at his feet. "I'm not sure I'll be doing anything that important."

"You are going to do wonderful things." She touched his arm. "My uncle says that God works through the people who come to that mission."

James opened his mouth to say something more but the young woman had already moved off toward a different gate. As he waited for other people to board he thought about what she had said. He prayed that he could make a difference by what he was doing. He showed his passport and boarding pass to the flight attendant.

She typed his itinerary into the computer. "First trip away from home?"

"Yes."

"You are heading a long distance." She looked up. "Are your traveling with a group?"

James shook his head. "No, I'm not traveling with a group."

"It must be a little scary to be going so far from home all by yourself."

James smiled at the flight attendant. "There may not be other people going with me but I'm not going alone."

Trinity Sunday
John 16:12-15

Always Together

John examined the sky. The blue was so perfect it seemed as if the whole scene was a painting. The clouds were light and fluffy and reminded him of cotton candy as they drifted past. He fidgeted in his seat wishing he could relax and enjoy the natural beauty of the day. Yet all he could think about was what he should do in the days to come and what would happen to him. A bird began singing in a nearby tree. John sat up to try and see it but as much as he strained he couldn't figure out which branch the song was coming from.

"It's beautiful, isn't it?"

The question came from a woman pulling along a pole holding an intravenous drip. Her hair was pulled back into a ponytail and the familiar medical identification band was wrapped around her wrist. Her hospital issue housecoat was pulled around her much as his was and she wore a pair of fuzzy pink slippers.

"Yeah. You might almost forget what we are doing here." He moved over on the bench to make room for her.

The woman smiled and sat down. John tried not to move too much in his seat. His eyes went back to the sky and tree but there was no way he could forget the diagnosis that had brought him to the hospital or escape the side effects of the treatment he was undergoing. A second bird began to sing from out of their view and soon the two were echoing each other's song.

"I would stay here all day if I could," the woman said softly.

"I hear you. It is certainly nicer than inside." John looked at the woman closely. "Have we met before?"

"We sat across from each other in the chapel service yesterday." She held out her hand. "I'm Paula."

"I'm John. You have a beautiful singing voice."

"Not nearly as wonderful as those birds. They are a real treat. I've never heard two of them sing together in all the time I've been coming out here."

"You come out often?"

"Every day that I am able." She counted on her fingers. "It'll be ten weeks for me. How long have you been in?"

John looked down at the band on his wrist that listed all his vital information. "Just finishing my first month."

"How is it going so far?"

"Okay. You?"

"Some days are better than others." She shrugged. "Hopefully the worst is behind me."

John glanced over at her. "Do you mind if I ask you a question?"

She kept watching the sky and the clouds. "Go ahead."

"Would you have gone through it if you had known how hard it was going to be?"

Paula turned toward him. "I really don't know. There are times I am glad that I opted for the treatment but other times when it is a bad week and I am so sick... well you know."

"Yeah, I do." John went back to looking at the clouds for a while. "I have to decide whether to go through another series."

"Well, are you?"

John shrugged. "I don't know what I should do. I'm not sure I could bear another month like the one I've had."

"Maybe the next one will be easier."

John looked in her eyes. "Was it like that for you?"

"The second month was actually worse." She tilted her head to one side. "The third though is going easier. I'm kind of glad we don't know what it's going to be like."

"Why do you say that?"

"I couldn't enjoy today if I knew tomorrow was going to be a rough day." She gestured all around her. "I'd miss all of this and I wouldn't have met you."

"Maybe that is why God hasn't answered my prayers." John looked at the ground. "I need to know what I am supposed to do."

Paula put her hand on his. "Maybe God is showing you something more important instead. If you know that God's love and grace is here for you today and if you know God understands and can help you, isn't that enough?"

"Maybe." John said. He wasn't convinced but Paula seemed so sure he started to hope that was all he needed.

Together they sat on the hospital roof watching the clouds drift past, feeling the gentle breeze on their faces, and listening to the songs of the birds in the trees. John felt a sense of peace embrace him. He still didn't know what tomorrow would bring but he realized that he wasn't anxious or nervous any longer.

Proper 4 / Pentecost 2 / Ordinary Time 9
Luke 7:1-10

Finding Faith

Sasha paced in front of the doors. She couldn't get the image of her sister getting on the plane out of her head — those curls and that smile as she waved and headed onto the walkway. Sasha wished she had never let Janice get on that flight. If only she had refused to let her go on the trip. If only she had taken the time off then she would be there with Janice. She stopped to look at the sign on the screen but it still said "delayed." Sascha sighed and started pacing again.

An airline official headed over to the desk and Sasha rushed forward with the other family members waiting in the blocked off section of the airport. He held up his hand at all the questions and demands for information.

"Sorry folks I don't have anything more than what the spokesperson said a few moment ago. The flight dropped off our radar screens and we still are trying to find out what happened to it." The man's face was haggard and worn. "What I need to do is confirm with family here who was on the flight to make sure our passenger lists are accurate."

"Why?" a woman from the back asked.

"Just a routine measure that the federal authorities want done to make sure that all avenues are covered."

"Do you suspect a terrorist attack?" A man at the front wanted to know. "Was there a bomb?"

"We have no indication that is what has happened. What I can tell you is that we do not have any reports of a crash so please stay hopeful. We are doing everything with the appropriate authorities to try and find out what has happened to your loved ones." The airline official pulled out a tablet and started tapping on the screen. "We appreciate your cooperation and will let you know any news as it becomes available."

Everyone went back to their places in the waiting area. Sasha tried to sit down but found herself fidgeting. She closed her eyes and tried to pray but kept seeing Janice's face. She opened her eyes and let out a loud sigh.

"It is hard not to know, isn't it?"

Sasha looked over at the small woman dressed in a sari sitting next to her and nodded. "My sister is on the plane."

"My husband is on his way back from the coast." the woman leaned in to her. "I know you do not know me but could you do something for me?"

"If I can."

"I see you have a cross. Are you a Christian?"

Sasha touched the necklace she wore. "Yes, I am."

"I am not a part of any church and do not even know if God would listen to me." The woman's eyes were wet with tears, "Could you pray for them?"

"I've been trying but I'm so upset I am finding it hard to pray. I'm so worried about my sister."

"But your God loves you and cares about you as a father cares for his children. Why do you find it hard to ask him to look after someone you love? Do you think he does not care about your sister?"

Sasha swallowed hard. "No. I believe God cares so much for us that he died as Jesus for our sakes."

"Then please pray for the people on that plane." The woman in the sari reached out her hand.

Sasha took her hand, bowed her head and prayed for the safety of the plane, for all the passengers, and for the officials looking for the missing flight. When she said *Amen* the woman in the sari threw her arms around her and held her tight.

"Thank you for being so kind to a stranger. I know they are all right now."

Sasha hugged her back. "I just prayed for them. I don't know what's happened."

"You have done all we can do." The woman let go of her and settled into the seat beside her. "But of course they will be all right. Your God is full of mercy and love. They will be cared for by that love no matter what has taken place."

The woman's words surrounded Sasha and she felt a calm and a peace fill her heart that she could not explain. They waited together in a center of calm amidst the anxiety and fear which surrounded them. When the airline official came out with a smile on his face to make an announcement that they had found the plane and everyone was all right the woman next to her clasped her hands and kissed her on the cheeks.

"Thank you for your prayer."

Sasha bowed her head slightly to the woman. "Thank you for helping me with my faith."

Proper 5 / Pentecost 3 / Ordinary Time 10
Luke 7:11-17

Resurrection Hope

Joan stared at the uneaten sandwich in her hands. She used to love coming to the park with David. He couldn't wait to rush through the gates so he could feed the pigeons, play around the fountain, or just sit beside her eating a snack and watching all the people. She felt her cheeks grow wet. She shouldn't have come here.

"Are you sad?" A little girl wearing jeans and a T-shirt with a yellow smiling sun on it was standing at one end of the bench.

"Excuse me?"

"You're crying." The girl took a step closer to her. "Are you sad?"

Joan wiped at her face and put her untouched lunch back in her bag. "I think I have something in my eye."

The little girl climbed onto the seat next to her, "Do you get things in your eyes a lot?"

Joan tried to smile and failed. "I guess so."

"I'm sorry."

Joan gathered up her things to leave. "I'll be all right."

"I'll pray for you."

Joan stopped and turned around. "Pardon?"

"When I go to bed tonight I'll talk to Jesus and tell him you're sad," the little girl said with a serious look on her face. "I'll ask him to help you."

"I'm fine." Joan touched her cheeks. "See? All better."

"That's what my daddy says but I can see him crying when he doesn't know I'm looking." The little girl slumped

129

in her seat. "He cries a lot since Mommy went away."

Joan sat back down on the bench. "Did she go somewhere?"

"She went up to heaven." The little girl pointed up at the sky. "Daddy says she isn't sick anymore and she is better there."

"I'm sorry," Joan said.

"Me too. Sometimes I wish she could come home." The little girl's eyes brimmed with tears. "Did your mommy go away too?"

Joan shook her head. "My little boy, David."

"Is that why you are sad?"

"Yes," Joan said softly. "I miss him."

"I miss Mommy too." The little girl's voice quivered. "Sometimes I worry that she is lonely in heaven without me there."

"I bet your mommy misses you, too. I think though she is happy that you are still here with your Daddy." Joan reached over and touched the little girl's hand. "I think that in heaven everything is okay. That's certainly what I hope and pray."

"Do you worry your little boy is lonely without you?"

Joan felt a rush of emotion and her eyes fill with tears. "I don't know."

"Do you think I could ask Jesus if my mommy and your little boy could keep each other company until we get to heaven?" The little girl held Joan's hand tightly. "That way I wouldn't worry so much about Mommy being lonely and you wouldn't have to worry so much about your little boy being lonely. Maybe it would help both of us."

Joan felt the drops fall from her eyes. "I think that would be a wonderful idea."

"I think I better go." The little girl pointed at a man on the other side of the park waving at her. "Daddy worries when I'm away from him for too long."

"Okay, dear." Joan squeezed her hand. "Thanks for talking to me."

"You're welcome. Maybe I will see you around. It's okay to be sad you know. Daddy told me that." The little girl started to run off toward her father but stopped and turned around. She looked Joan squarely in the eye. "Jesus is always ready to listen if you ever need to talk. Daddy told me that too."

Joan smiled and wiped her cheeks as the little girl rushed across the park into the waiting arms of her father. She watched the people passing by her for a few moments and then slowly unpacked her lunch. She took a couple of bites and found herself thinking of the last time that she and David were in the park.

He had been so happy that afternoon. He had the biggest smile she had ever seen on his face and squealed with delight as he fed the pigeons. She remembered him saying as they left to go home that it was the best day in his life. For the first time since the funeral Joan finally accepted that David was safe and at peace in God's care. Joan bowed her head to ask God to help her through the pain and then she sat in the park and let herself remember and weep for a while.

Proper 6 / Pentecost 4 / Ordinary Time 11
Luke 7:36—8:3

Witness of the Sinful

Joanna slipped into the back of the church just as the opening prayer began. She ignored the people around her and focused on the service. She sang the hymns reverently and listened to the message carefully. She felt God's forgiveness and love surrounding her. She lost herself in the words and music.

She normally rushed out during the last verse of the final hymn but the words were so lovely that she didn't realize that it was over until the pastor was coming down the aisle. She tried to dart past him but he stuck out his hand to say good morning. She muttered something in response and realized he was blocking her way out.

"Could you stay for a moment?" he asked.

She nodded and slunk into the corner. She watched the pleasant people in their Sunday best speaking with the pastor before they went home. She recognized some of them as successful leaders in the community. She looked down at her old shirt and scuffed shoes. She sighed as she waited for the pastor. She didn't fit in at this church and it was obvious. He was going to tell her that she had to go somewhere else. Her stomach become knots as the last people went through the door and as the pastor turned toward her.

"You're Joanna Kinsman, aren't you?" The pastor took off the microphone he had worn for the service. "You live in the east section buildings, don't you?"

Her heart raced. "Yes."

"This is kind of awkward." The pastor rubbed the back of his neck. "I heard you speak at a meeting a while back over in the community center."

A weight pressed down on her shoulders. He knew her past. "Yes, I'm a recovering addict. I did some terrible things in that part of my life."

"It was an open meeting otherwise I wouldn't bring it up." The pastor looked embarrassed. "I'm sorry I really don't know how to ask this and I apologize if this seems blunt."

"It's okay, I'll not bother you again." Joanna headed toward the door. "I'll find somewhere else to worship."

"What?"

Joanna stopped. "You're going to ask me to leave, aren't you?"

"Why would I do that?"

She gestured at her clothes. "You know my history and I'm not the sort of person you want in your church. I get that."

The pastor shook his head. "You're as welcome here as any other child of God."

Her brow furrowed. "But you know my past."

"I heard you speak about how the love of Jesus helped you stay clean and how the forgiveness let you start a new life." The pastor looked her in the eyes. "Your story was inspirational."

She shrugged. "It's nothing special."

"I disagree. You know God's grace and mercy intimately. That's why I wanted to talk with you."

"I don't understand," she said. "You don't want me to leave this church?"

"Heavens, no. I want you to speak to our senior youth group."

Joanna let the relief that she was not being asked to leave sink in for a moment. Then she frowned. "I'm not good at speeches."

"I disagree. I heard you speak about your life and finding Christ and it was direct and real. What I want you to do is simply talk to them."

"I'm not a very good role model. You should find someone living a better life. Someone for them to look up to." Joanna pointed back toward where the coffee hour was happening. "I'm sure you've got a church full of good people."

"I've got a youth group who need to know that God's love and grace can change them," the pastor said. "I want the teens to hear about how important it is to let Christ into their hearts. I want someone who knows grace and love to witness to them."

Joanna rubbed her chin. "There are things I wouldn't be comfortable telling them."

"Can you share how God has helped you?"

"Easily," Joanna said. "When do you want me to speak to them?"

"They meet every Sunday after service. Pick one and you can have the time with them."

Joanna looked at her watch. "How about now?"

The pastor clapped his hands together. "Excellent. Can I ask one more thing?"

Joanna's eyes narrowed. "What?"

"Would it be okay for me to sit in and listen?" He gave her a big smile. "The last time I heard you witness it touched me deeply."

Joanna felt her face flush and nodded. As she followed the pastor further into the church she said a prayer of thanks for the surprising nature of grace. A moment ago, she was sure that she was going to be told to leave and now she was being asked to lead others into a deeper faith. Her eyes filled with tears as she realized the God's grace was still at work in her life.

Proper 7 / Pentecost 5 / Ordinary Time 12
Luke 8:26-39

A New Life

Will lived on the streets and borrowed, begged, and stole what he needed to survive. He was always hungry but when he got some money his first stop was the liquor store. Everyone kept their distance from him and Will liked it that way. Honestly though, it was the only way he had known for many years.

One day Will was sprawled next to the dumpster behind the liquor store trying to get some shade because his head was pounding. A man he had never seen came around the corner and knelt next to him.

"Go away," Will snarled.

"You must be Will." The man held out his hand. "My name is Jim."

Will rolled his eyes. "I don't care. Leave me alone. I'm not interested in whatever it is that you're selling."

"Why do you think that I am selling something?" Jim asked.

"Because you do gooders always have something you think will make me better," Will growled. "I'm not some lost puppy you can find a home for and go away feeling good about yourself."

Jim laughed. "I would never mistake you for a lost puppy. I just wanted to say hello and introduce myself."

Will scowled. "Why should I care?"

"You don't have to," Jim said. "Just know that I care."

"Wonderful. My life is complete." Will slumped down. "Now go away."

Jim stood up and went back around the corner.

The next day as Will was digging through the dumpster behind the bakery he saw Jim coming down the alley.

"What are you doing here?" Will asked.

"Looking for you."

Will frowned. "How did you know I'd be here?"

"I assumed you had to eat some time and I heard this was the day they throw out the stale bread. I assumed you'd be along."

"I'm not big on sharing," Will said.

"Lucky for you I am." Jim opened his bag and held out a sandwich. Will's mouth began to water. He grabbed it and wolfed it down.

"This doesn't mean anything to me," Will declared as he took the carton of cold milk that Jim offered.

"That's okay," Jim said before he left. "It does to me."

Will wasn't surprised when Jim was waiting for him on the following day next to the donation bin outside of the goodwill.

"Buzz off. I'm looking for something warm to wear." Will noticed the bag slung across Jim's shoulder. "The nights are getting colder."

"They certainly are getting chilly." Jim paused. "If I said I knew of a bed open at the mission would you be interested?"

"The religious place?" Will shook his head. "No way. You can go try to save someone else."

"I don't save people." Jim handed a sleeping bag to Will. "I just tell them about the one who does."

Will looked at the package in his arms and tried to think of something sharp and biting to say but Jim had already wandered away.

The night was cold but Will was comfortable in the sleeping bag. He was sound asleep when the police officers told him to move along. They shook him to make sure he was all right but Will thought they were trying to steal his stuff and punched and kicked at them. He spent the rest of the night behind bars.

Will was surprised when Jim appeared outside of the cell. "What are you doing here?"

"I visit here," Jim said. "What are you doing here?"

Jim listened as Will explained the events leading to his arrest. Then Jim disappeared for a moment. He came back with the officer who had put Will in the cell. The officer unlocked the door and told Will he was free to go and that there would be no charges.

"Why did you help me?" Will asked as they walked outside together.

"Because I was helped myself when I was in trouble." Jim started off in the opposite direction from Will. "See you around."

"What did you do?" Will called out.

Jim stopped. "I'm hungry and going to get something to eat. You're welcome to join me."

Will was going to say no but his stomach chose that moment to rumble. He picked up his sleeping bag and headed off with Jim. The meal they had was simple and plain. The conversation they had was deep and personal. Jim talked about how he had once lived on the streets and his troubles with the law and drugs. He told Will about the difference Jesus had made and the new life that was possible through Christ.

Will listened carefully. He wanted to scoff and ignore what the other man was telling him. Yet he found that the words Jim shared touched him like nothing else had before. For on that morning Will's life changed forever.

Proper 8 / Pentecost 6 / Ordinary Time 13
Luke 9:51-62

Being Ready

There once was a group of well-meaning and compassionate people who saw that there was a great spiritual hunger in their community. They realized they needed a place where the good news of God would be proclaimed and outreach to the poor could be organized. So the well-meaning and compassionate people gathered together and discussed what they needed to do in order to be a church.

They realized there was a great deal for them to decide — what their worship would be like, what mission work they would undertake, and how their church committees would be organized. They wanted their church to succeed so they carefully began to discuss and explore all the possibilities. The initial gathering extended to regular weekly meetings and subcommittees were struck to consider every detail. Time passed and it seemed they were no closer to being a church.

"We must get the spiritual poor and impoverished to come to our meetings," announced a concerned individual. "That way they can see how wonderful it would be to have a church in the community and that would motivate us."

Everyone agreed that it would be inspiring to let the people they would reach know about their great plans and intentions. It was also noted that they would soon be reaching their first year anniversary of planning and meeting in the community about the possibility of becoming a church. Someone wondered if they might invite all the people they wanted to serve to be with them to mark that milestone.

The longer the idea was discussed though the more the consensus grew that it would be premature to share what they had been doing. After all there was still so much work to be done. So the whole matter was referred to an ad hoc committee in the hopes that after a few years it might come back to the main group.

"We could hold fund raisers and get some money so we can pay people for the time they are taking," someone suggested. "Because becoming a church is a complicated process."

There was a great deal of conversation about this point. Everyone agreed that their time was precious so a vote was taken to put everything on hold until they raised enough money to keep funding their efforts to consider the possibility of becoming a church. There was a great deal of procedural wrangling over the exact wording of the motion. As well there were a great number of impassioned speeches which all said the same thing about how important the work they would be doing would be as soon as they had the money to pay themselves to get about considering how to do the work.

"Why can't we just be a church now?" asked a voice from the back.

Everyone turned to look at the man raising the question. No one really knew who the man was although some said he had been there at the first meeting. It was also thought that he had missed a great deal of the work they had done in discussing what model they should adopt to govern themselves. That led to some whispered comments about how rude this man was in asking such a question of the good and compassionate people who had been working so diligently at getting them ready to be a church.

"Well of course we're not ready." one person explained on behalf of the others. "We have so much more to do. There is a great deal involved in being a church."

"What could be simpler than worshiping God and following in the way Jesus calls us to follow?" the man asked.

"But we need to plan and discuss and consider," another person said. "Otherwise we might not do it as well as we could do."

The man looked at the nodding heads around the room. "Don't you care about the people in the community who need to hear the good news and are hungry for the hope and peace which a church can bring them?"

A third person shot to his feet. "We care very deeply. That is why we are going to make sure that we do this right. With enough money to study and consider how to be a church we will someday be the best church possible."

The caring and compassionate people went back to discussing their need for money and how best to raise those funds. They set up a number of subcommittees and were so busy discussing timetables and considering possibilities that they never noticed the man leaving their meeting.

They never saw the man go out into the community and talk to those on the streets about the love and mercy of God. They were so busy with what they thought was important that they never saw the man caring for the sick and inviting the lost to come and be a part of the kingdom of God. They never saw the church which formed in their community as people committed their lives to following the teachings and way of the living Christ who walked among them.

Proper 9 / Pentecost 7 / Ordinary Time 14
Luke 10:1-11, 16-20

Grounded in Faith

Paula was a Christian. She accepted that Jesus Christ had come to earth to show the grace of God and bring salvation to all of humanity. She had faith that her sins were forgiven and that through Christ she was offered a new life. She listened and watched for the Holy Spirit at work around her. Paula worked hard at living out her faith each and every day.

She was a member of her church. She attended every Sunday and shared her gift of music in the choir. She took part in the fellowship activities that happened after church and never missed a time when there was a dinner or a potluck. She read her Bible each day and prayed when she first awoke and just before she went to sleep. She also made sure that she dutifully tithed her money to God's work. Paula did all of these things with care and attention, for she took pride in her spiritual activities.

Yet she could not shake the feeling that her faith was a pale shadow of what it should be. Paula often felt like she was simply going through the motions. She struggled to maintain her routines and spiritual practices. She remembered the faith of her grandmother, who always had such certainty, such vibrancy, and such joy as she worshiped and served. Paula worried that her faith was incomplete.

So she did more. She went outside her comfort zone and volunteered for the governing board of the church. She agreed to teach Sunday school. For a time she found herself excited and inspired by these new activities. She was able to offer more of her gifts and skills to help her church. She enjoyed getting to know the young people and working with them helped her to see the stories of the Bible in a new light.

Yet over time even those things began to feel like chores. She didn't dislike them and knew that they were meaningful but they no longer brought her the joy or excitement that they once had. She started to wonder if God was unhappy with what she was doing.

Paula volunteered at the local mission. She worked with the poor in the city and helped sort clothes and donated cans of food in the backroom. The work was tedious but she knew that it was essential when she saw the people lining up for help each day. She found meaning and purpose in her outreach work and came to understand a world which she knew nothing about. She felt satisfied that she was doing something she was supposed to do.

Yet over time even this activity, which she knew was important and definitely ministry was not bringing her joy or excitement. All of which caused Paula to question herself and her faith. For she was really beginning to believe that God was not happy with what she was doing in her life.

She knew her Bible, she prayed, she tithed, and she took time for worship. She was learning, she was serving, she was doing everything she was supposed to do but joy was missing in her spiritual life. She wanted the faith she had seen her grandmother live out. She wanted the certainty that God was with her.

Paula poured out her frustration and anxiety to her mother one afternoon after church. She explained all her activities, all her faithful service, and all the emptiness she was feeling. She wanted to know what else she should be doing to please God.

"Why do you think you need to please God?" her mother asked. "Why do you think your activities will help you find joy and satisfaction?"

"Because they did for grandmother," Paula replied. "She was always certain in her faith, always joyful no matter how tedious or mind-numbing the task. She rejoiced in God's presence from the moment she woke until the moment she slept. I do all the things she did but find myself miserable."

"Actually you are doing more than you grandmother ever did," her mother said. "The difference is that your grandmother knew joy and meaning in her life and then went to work. You on the other hand are trying to find joy and meaning through your work."

"How did she know joy and meaning before she began?"

"She knew God accepted and loved her as she was." Her mother smiled. "With every action she took your grandmother responded to God's love with love of her own."

Paula took those words to heart and let her life change. She still prayed, went to church, served on the board, taught Sunday school, and volunteered at the mission. Sometimes the work was hard, tedious, and she found it stressful. Yet at those times she stopped herself and remembered why she was doing all of those things. Not because she needed God to love her but because she was loved by God.

Proper 10 / Pentecost 8 / Ordinary Time 15
Luke 10:25-37

Being a Neighbor

Fiona rolled up the windows, locked the doors, and stared straight ahead as she waited for the light to turn green. A man carrying a sign saying "Hungry, Please Help" walked past her car holding out a scruffy baseball cap. When the light changed she sped away and breathed a sigh of relief.

Her mind though kept replaying the encounter. Enjoying her morning coffee and donut, she thought about the sign the man carried. Sitting through the morning meeting, she wondered what events had put him on the streets. Entering data and finishing up reports, she started to question the way she had acted.

"Something the matter, Fi?" Joan dropped a stack of files on her desk.

"Sorry." Fiona managed a weak smile. "Just lost in thought."

"I hope at least he's cute."

"Who?"

"Whoever it is that has you half here and half there." Joan grinned. "Did you meet him when you were out at the movies with your nieces last night? Did your heart pound and you know at first sight that he's the one?"

"You read way too many romance novels." Fiona rolled her eyes. "I took two ten year olds out to dinner with a gift card I got as a present last month and then to a family-friendly movie."

"Spoil sport," Joan said. "So who is he?"

"Someone I saw on the way to work." Fiona held up her hand. "And no it isn't romantic in the least. He was begging at the intersection of Main and First."

"I know who you mean. He's creepy." Joan shivered. "I wish the cops would move him along. You didn't encourage him, did you?"

"No, I didn't make eye contact and made sure my doors were locked."

"You can never be too careful," Joan said. "So why are you still thinking about him?"

"His sign said he was hungry." Fiona touched the cross on her necklace. "Maybe I should have given him some money."

"He would have drank it or smoked it. I'm sure it's just a scam. I have a friend who told me those beggars make better money than we do."

Fiona thought about the man's haggard face and sunken eyes. "I guess so."

Joan put her hand on Fiona's shoulder. "Trust me, Fi, the money is better in your pocket than his. Speaking of that, you want the normal lunch order?"

Fiona nodded and turned her attention back to work. She tried to tell herself that the man probably would have wasted any money she gave him on drugs or that he didn't need it. Yet she kept seeing his face and eyes. The image didn't leave her as she finished work for the day and started out toward the parking lot. She opened the door for a friend who attended her church.

"Chris, do you pass the corner of First and Main?"

"Not normally," he said. "I can give you a drive if you need one though."

Joan shook her head. "No, it's not that but there is a fellow begging at that corner I ignored. Was that the right thing to do?"

"I always ask what would Jesus do." Chris paused for a moment. "I suppose he would help."

"But how?"

"I guess he would feed the man if he said he was hungry." Chris' phone began to ring. "Sorry Fi, but I need to take this."

Fiona felt conflicted as she drove home. She wanted to help, felt that she should help, but she didn't want to do the wrong thing. She came to the intersection and saw the man standing with his hat in hand and the sign saying that he was hungry. Waiting at the red light she reached into her purse to see if she had any money and touched the gift card. She pulled it out with the receipt saying how much was left on it. She rolled down the window and gestured for the man to come over.

"Are you really hungry?" she asked.

"I haven't eaten since yesterday," he replied. "Anything you can spare would help."

She handed him the gift card. "There is still twenty dollars and change left on this. Go and get yourself some supper and some breakfast tomorrow."

The man's eyes filled with tears. "God bless you."

The light changed and Fiona drove away. She was still thinking about the man and his situation as she pulled into her driveway. She was going to phone the pastor at the church. Maybe he knew of a shelter or other help that could get the man back on his feet. As she put the key in the front door of her house she felt a calm descend upon her that she had not felt all day.

Proper 11 / Pentecost 9 / Ordinary Time 16
Luke 10:38-42

Two Paths

Julie and Sue were inseparable from the time they were born. They shared a room growing up and loved to play together. As teenagers they joined the same activities and clubs. As women they raised their children in houses on the same street. When their families had grown and after their husbands had died they moved into an apartment together.

They were both women with good and caring hearts and tried their best to live moral and upright lives. They went to church together on Sunday and helped out in the women's fellowship whenever there was a sale or a rally. Everyone who saw them said they were like two peas in a pod. Yet the sisters were very different.

Julie was carefree and loved to dance and sing. She was skilled with her hands and everything she touched turned into a beautiful work of art. Her laughter was infectious and she enjoyed being outside no matter what the season.

Sue on the other hand was more serious and thoughtful. The medium for her expression was words and she loved to debate and examine ideas. She had a smile that lit up a room and loved nothing better than spending time with people in conversation.

One day when the work was finished around the house Julie turned to her sister. "Let's go for a walk and enjoy the evening."

"We did what you wanted yesterday," Sue said. "The library is hosting a world-renowned speaker tonight. We can always walk later."

Julie's face fell. "There is another storm predicted for the morning. The next few days will be terrible."

"I suppose we could walk to the lecture if we hurry." Sue took her hand. "You are going to love what the speaker is going to talk about."

Julie doubted she would enjoy any lecture but seeing the excitement on her sister's face she simply nodded.

They walked arm in arm on the way to the library. Julie delighted in pointing out to Sue the birds in the trees and naming the flowers as they passed. Sue looked at her watch but saw the joy in Julie's face and said nothing. Sue suddenly stopped and shushed her sister.

"What's that noise?" Sue asked.

Julie tilted her head. "I don't hear anything."

"You were always a bit deaf," Sue said. "It is kind of a high pitched warble."

"That doesn't sound like any bird I know. Maybe one has been blown into our area by the coming storm." Julie looked at the path that headed into the woods. "I wish we had time to search for it."

"Let's have a look," Sue said well aware that they were going to be late. "I think we can make it to the library this way."

The two sisters headed into a little grove of trees. Occasionally Sue would stop and listen for the sound of the rare bird and direct her sister this way or that way. Julie would point out things along the path and marvel at the colors and interconnection of the small little forest.

When it was too dark to see they finally emerged just beyond the library. People were streaming out the doors.

"I think we have missed your lecture," Julie said. "I'm sorry."

"That's okay." Sue hugged her sister's to her. "I wish we could have seen that bird. I would've loved to see you paint it."

"But we agreed that we would go to do what you wanted tonight and listen to the speaker." Julie turned to her sister. "What was the lecture about?"

" 'Finding God around you,' " Sue replied.

"I feel awful that I held us up with all my wanting to see a bird and all my chattering on about flowers and trees."

Sue smiled and took her sister's arm. "There will be other lectures on other days. It was nice to spend the time admiring God's handiwork and watching you get inspiration for your art."

"But it isn't fair to you," Julie protested. "We agreed to do what you wanted. You didn't enjoy the day like I did."

Sue shook her head. "You don't get it do you? I enjoyed our walk. No words a stranger could speak to me about seeing God in the world could compare to the time we just spent where I got to see God through your eyes."

"But —"

Sue put her finger over her sister's mouth. "There are greater things than getting your own way."

Julie slowly nodded and together the sisters turned toward home. "What do you think the speaker would have lectured about?"

Sue began to describe the articles and books written by the lecturer who had spoken at the library. With each word Sue shared Julie began to understand why her sister had been so patient and selfless that evening. For to her surprise, her sister's passion inspired her and enriched her faith.

Proper 12 / Pentecost 10 / Ordinary Time 17
Luke 11:1-13

Learning to Pray

Cora sat down in the back of the empty chapel. She took a deep breath and closed her eyes. She tried to clear her mind and let the words come to her but nothing happened. She took another deep breath and tried again. Still the words didn't come.

She looked up at the cross at the front and felt her cheeks grow wet. This wasn't fair. She never had a problem praying before. She just paused and the words flowed from her. She always felt the presence of God in her life even when things were difficult or uncertain. So what was wrong with her now? Why was God silent? Why couldn't she pray anymore?

Cora shifted in her seat and folded her hands together. She closed her eyes so tight that the tears fell even faster. She tried to pray, wanted to pray, but nothing happened. For the first time in her life she felt lost and alone. She put her face in her hands and felt the sobs wrack her body. A hand touched her shoulder and she jumped in her seat.

"Sorry, I didn't mean to startle you." A woman was standing next to her. Her face was wrinkled and her hair was white. "I thought the chapel was empty."

Cora got up and wiped at her cheeks. "That's okay I'll leave."

"Are you okay?"

Cora shrugged. "I guess so."

"If you don't mind me saying you really don't look that okay." The woman sat down and patted the seat next to her.

"I can't imagine such sobs coming from a person without some serious troubles weighing down her heart."

Cora paused and then sat. "I can't pray. I have always been able to pray but for some reason the words just don't come."

"Too distracted by things happening in your life?"

Cora shook her head. "No, I just feel my prayers are empty."

"I can see how that would be frustrating but the emotion I saw was real despair, why?"

Cora looked at her feet. "I think I may have lost my faith."

"You're trying to pray which says to me you still have your faith." The woman gestured around. "If you had no faith you wouldn't be looking for God any longer."

"You really think so?" Cora said.

"I know so. Does it feel like you're alone and God is nowhere to be found?"

"It does."

The woman nodded. "I can remember how unpleasant that feels."

"It's happened to you?"

"A couple of times." The woman turned toward the cross. "One day everything was wonderful and I knew God was near me the moment I spoke. The next I felt alone in the universe and my prayers seemed to bounce off the ceiling instead of going to God."

"What did you do? Did you keep praying?"

"I did." The woman turned to look Cora in the eyes. "But I'll tell you the truth it remained hard for a while."

Cora sighed. "I wish I could pray and feel God's presence."

The woman patted her hand. "All I can say is to keep praying."

"I can't find the words."

The woman opened up a pew bible and pointed to a page. "Then use the words that Jesus gave us. Use the psalms. Above all keep praying."

Cora took the Bible in her hand and looked at the words of the Lord's Prayer. "Thanks. I'll try."

The woman got up to leave.

"Wait." Cora stood. "I'll go so you can do whatever you came here to do before I distracted you."

The woman smiled. "I think I did it."

"I don't understand."

"I was passing by and felt that the most important thing for me to do was come into this chapel." The woman shrugged. "I had no idea why. I thought I was supposed to pray or meditate but now I think the Holy Spirit was telling me to come here to speak with you."

"I'm glad you did," Cora said.

"I am as well." The woman took hold of the door handle. "You've blessed me richly."

Cora frowned. "But I didn't do anything but tell you my troubles."

"True, but in doing so you let me be the answer God was giving to you." The woman opened the door. "For even when we can't hear God, God hears us and answers with grace."

Cora sat down as the chapel door closed behind the woman. She held the Bible in her hands, took a deep breath, and started to pray "Our Father..."

Proper 13 / Pentecost 11 / Ordinary Time 18
Luke 12:13-21

Being Rich

There once was a man named Timothy. Timothy was born into a loving home where his parents gave him every opportunity that they could. His father held down two jobs to provide Timothy with the best food, medical care, and education. His mother worked with him tirelessly tutoring him in his subjects and helping him to excel in the arts and at sports. As he was growing up they taught him that the most important thing in life is to be rich.

Timothy saw his parents efforts and he worked hard. He took advantage of the opportunities that they gave him and excelled academically and socially. People liked Timothy and he always did his best in his studies and extracurricular activities. Some things came easy to him but others required him to find help which he did without hesitation. For Timothy knew that the best things in life were not easily achieved but required dedication and persistence. He wasn't afraid to put in the long hours of practice and study that was needed to excel.

Timothy went on to university and found that his hard work and natural ability allowed him to become an expert in his chosen field. When he finished his degrees he was offered his dream job with a large company. He took the position and with long hours and dedication was soon offered the chance to rise in the ranks. He decided, though, to form his own company so that he could choose the work he was taking and so that his efforts would bring him the most reward. For he still believed that the most important thing in life was to be rich.

He met a woman and fell in love. He moved into his dream house in the part of the city he had always wanted to live. He had two children, a boy and a girl, whom he loved dearly and because of his skill and work habits was able to spend time with them as they grew. He had good friends and neighbors and cherished the people who were part of his life. Timothy still believed that the most important thing in life was to be rich but he had watched too many men his age lose their health and family through overwork and pledged not to do the same in his life.

So Timothy was careful to watch his diet and to exercise. He made sure to spend time with his wife and family and no matter what else was happening ensured they were part of his day. He never betrayed a friend or broke a confidence and tried to be honorable in both his business and personal life. Timothy was making more money than he had ever dreamed in a career that he excited him while being happily married with a family he adored. Timothy was rich in every way that he could imagine and know. Everyone thought he had the perfect life and he thought so too.

Yet Timothy wasn't happy. He felt that there was something missing even though he couldn't see anything wrong with his life. He liked his career, he had plenty of money, he had a great marriage and good children, and he had his health.

Timothy concentrated more on himself. Because of his careful saving and conscientious attitude toward work he could take time to travel and to pursue interests and hobbies. He took vacations and saw all the places he wanted to see. He learned new skills and enrolled in courses to improve himself. While doing that Timothy realized he could give more to his family as well.

He made sure that his children had every opportunity he could provide. He planned weekly family activities to places and events around the country. He went out of his way to make sure every birthday, anniversary, and holiday was the best he could make it. He supported his wife in her interests and work and was as loving a husband as he could be.

Yet Timothy still could not shake the emptiness he felt. It was as if he was missing something essential, something vital in his life. Even the things that delighted him, his abilities, his education, his success, and his achievements seemed to be a shadow of what they could be.

Timothy was rich in every way he knew. Yet despite all his possessions, despite his great family and circle of friends, despite being able to do whatever he wanted to do and to indulge his every whim, Timothy was poor in the eyes of God.

Proper 14 / Pentecost 12 / Ordinary Time 19
Luke 12:32-40

Sharing the Wealth

"So what's important to you?" Sally knew she should have kept quiet the moment the words left her mouth. She looked at the reactions of the girls at the sleepover. Tina was looking off in the distance and Allie was struggling to keep her eyes open but June and Peggy were frowning. Sally looked at the floor. "It really doesn't matter I guess."

"Of course it doesn't matter." June ran her fingers through her long black hair. "What matters is what's popular. It would be wrong to like things that are, well, wrong because you don't ever want to be one of those people."

Peggy tittered, Allie nodded, and Sally felt her face grow warm. She should have kept her mouth shut. She was lucky that June invited her over since she'd only lived in the neighborhood for a few months. The other girls had known each other for years.

"What other people, June?" Tina asked.

June rolled her eyes. "You know the wrong people."

"I don't know what you mean by the wrong people. I know people who don't agree with me and who like different things than me but that doesn't make them wrong." Tina pointed at the poster on the wall. "That singer isn't my favorite. Does that make me the wrong people?"

June shook her head. "No, the last songs she put out were lame. It's okay to like other music."

"Then I think Sally's question is a good one. What's important to us?" Tina put her hand on her chin. "I guess my family and my friends are important to me. What about you?"

"My phone," Peggy chirped up. "I couldn't imagine not having my phone."

Everyone laughed.

"Could you live without it though?" Tina asked.

"Absolutely not." Peggy frowned for a moment. "Well I guess I could. Last year when I went to see my Nana there was no cell service and I did okay for a week. I was so bored it wasn't funny but I survived."

"I couldn't live without Puddles," Allie said. "My dog is always there for me."

"Pets are important. I don't know what I would do without Mittens." June reached down and petted the cat curled up on the floor. "I could live without the fish downstairs though."

"Well what about you, Sally?" Tina asked. "What's important to you?"

Sally looked around the room at the girls waiting for her answer. She desperately wanted them to like her. She so wanted to be part of this group. She didn't want to say the wrong thing but she knew what she had to say. She took a deep breath.

"God. I couldn't live without my faith."

The room went deathly silent.

Tina looked off in the distance again. Allie's eyes went wide and darted from side to side. Peggy put down her phone and stared at Sally. June's mouth grew hard. Sally knew her face was beet red. She had blown it. She should have said something else. She should have said anything else. Now no one was ever going to speak to her again. She was going to spend all of her days eating lunch alone in the cafeteria. The seconds dragged on into minutes.

Tina cleared her throat. "What church do you go to?"

Well that was it. She was going to be made fun of. Yet a part of her knew that what she had done was faithful and she felt that it was right. God was important to her, the most important part of her life and she wasn't going to hide it. She felt a boldness come over her and looked Tina squarely in the eyes.

"St. Peter's over on Riverside."

"I don't think I've ever seen you there," Tina said. "What service do you go to?"

"My mom likes to go to the early one."

Tina nodded. "That's why. My parents prefer to sleep in so we go to the late service."

"We go to First over on Main Street," Peggy said. "That was the church my grandmother always attended."

"Grace Memorial," Allie said. "Although we don't go as much as we used to since my dad works shifts."

Everyone realized that June hadn't said anything. She blushed slightly. "We go the cathedral at Christmas with my grandfather. But I guess I really don't know much about God beyond the baby Jesus."

The conversation then continued with each girl telling what she liked best about her church and what it was that interested her about God and religion. As they went around the room sharing their faith, Sally whispered a prayer of thanks that her witness had led to an evening with new friends that was not only fun but meaningful.

Proper 15 / Pentecost 13 / Ordinary Time 20
Luke 12:49-56

The Difficult Way

Andy put his car keys in his pocket and crept out of his room. He was careful to sidestep the squeaky floorboard in the hallway and moved as silently as possible down the stairs. He breathed a sigh of relief as he saw the front door.

His mother came out of the kitchen with a mug in her hand. "Just where do you think that you are going at this hour of the morning?"

Andy sighed. "You know where I am going, Mom."

"I want to hear it from your lips."

"I'm going to church."

She scowled at him. "I don't like it."

Andy closed his eyes. He was getting tired of this argument anytime there was something at the church.

"Most mothers would be pleased there son is going off to church on Sunday morning instead of hanging around the house sleeping off a hangover like I used to do."

She grunted. "At least then you would have some friends."

"I have friends at church." Andy forced a smile. "You are always welcome to come and meet them."

"Bah." She shook her head. "I never had time for church and I don't know why you do either. It's just a bunch of mumbo jumbo."

Andy held up his hands. "I don't want to fight about this again, Mom. They are good people at the church and Pastor Joel is a great speaker."

"Wasting time is what you are doing. They are all hypocrites you know." His mother put her mug on the table. "Every last one of them is no better than I am despite the 'holier than thou' attitude that you've picked up from them."

"This is important to me," Andy said. "I am going to church this morning."

"But why? We used to go to church at Christmas and that was always good enough. Why do you have to go every week?"

"It makes my life complete. There are great people there and I feel that being part of the church is what God wants me to do."

"God wants you to respect your mother. I know that's in the Bible."

"I do respect you, Mom." Andy gestured around. "After Dad died I stayed here to help you. Most of my friends have moved into their own places."

"If you loved me then you would stop going to church."

Andy shook his head. "Church is important to me and I'm going to keep going."

His mother scowled. "You're not the same person you were before you started going to that place every week."

"Thank you, Mom." Andy smiled. "That is the best compliment you could have paid me."

"I didn't mean it as one."

"I'm taking it as one though. I was a selfish man who was living from day to day without any real purpose. Now with Jesus in my life I am living the way I'm supposed to."

His mother stamped her foot. "If you live in my house you have to follow my rules."

Andy took a deep breath. "I have always respected you and what you taught me."

"I've had enough of this church foolishness from you," his mother said. "I won't have some holy roller who doesn't listen to me living under my roof. If you live here you will not go to church."

"Is that your final word?" Andy paused. "You really forbid me from going to church if I live here?"

She crossed her arms. "Absolutely."

Andy turned around and slowly walked back up the stairs. His mother grinned and clapped her hands together as he disappeared out of view. She turned to go back into the kitchen when she heard a squeak from the upstairs hallway. Andy had a suitcase in one hand and a duffel bag slung over his shoulder.

She met him at the bottom of the stairs. "What are you doing?"

"I'm moving out."

"You would leave me alone in this world?" Tears began to run down her cheeks. "Is that what your Jesus is all about leaving poor widowed mothers alone?"

"I'm not going to play any more games with you, Mom." Andy stepped past her. "I have my cell phone with me if there is an emergency."

"Is this what you want?" His mother shouted as he opened the door "I'm not going to stand in your way if this is what you really want."

"No, this is not what I want." Andy stopped in the doorway. "But I think maybe this is for the best. I'll call you next week to see how you're doing."

Andy stepped out of the house and headed toward his car. His heart was heavy but he had no doubt that each step he took was the way he was supposed to go.

Pentecost 16 / Pentecost 14 / Ordinary Time 21
Luke 13:10-17

The Rule of Love

Agnes stood before the gathered members of the women's group. "I did and I would do it again in an instant."

The room erupted in murmuring and whispers. Many of the women glared and shook their heads in disapproval.

"Agnes that was not your food to give away. That was donated for the church sale." Bernice said. "You had no right to give it to that man."

"You should have told him to get out. He and his kind are not welcome here," Cheryl muttered. "He smells."

There were mutters of agreement and a couple of whispers about how the police should have been called because that man was probably up to no good.

"His name is Charlie," Agnes said.

The room went quiet.

"What?" Bernice asked.

"The man I gave the food to has a name." Agnes looked around the room. "His name is Charlie Everett and he grew up not far from here."

"Where?" Sadie piped up. "I don't remember any Everett family in the neighborhood."

"He's Hazel Everett's boy."

"You mean Hazel who lived on the corner?" Sadie rubbed her chin. "Yeah, I remember her boy. Quiet and kept to himself. That's him?"

Agnes nodded.

"I don't care what his name is or who his mother was," Bernice said. "You gave food that wasn't yours to give.

That's wrong."

"Charlie knocked on the door of the church and said he was hungry." Agnes put her hands on her hips. "What was I supposed to do?"

"Turn him away. Tell him to come back and speak to the pastor on Sunday. Go talk to his social worker or whoever else deals with people like him," Bernice said. "He is not our problem."

"He can't get in to see his worker at the VA until midweek. He was hungry now so I fed him."

Bernice stomped her foot. "You gave away food that would have earned this church much needed money. Money we don't have because your actions cheated us of those funds."

The murmuring against Agnes rose in intensity. Sadie stepped forward and raised her hand and everyone was quiet.

"Hazel Everett's boy had an appointment at the Veterans Administration you said?"

Agnes nodded. "He was over in Afghanistan."

Bernice's face went red "That doesn't matter —"

Sadie cut her off. "It mattered when your William went off to Vietnam and it mattered when my dear husband was over in Europe."

Bernice closed her mouth.

"That just means he should be the government's problem and not ours," Cheryl muttered.

The whole group turned to glare at her.

She shrank back. "I meant that the government should do a better job of caring for our veterans."

Agnes cleared her throat. "All I know is that he was hungry and knocked on the door of the church. I talked to him and gave him some food from the sale to tide him over until he can get in to see his worker."

Bernice shook her head. "That's not the point. The money was for the church —"

163

"— and the church is about loving people as Jesus loves," Agnes said. "I won't apologize for him thinking that this congregation cares about him."

There were a few mutters but most people nodded their heads.

"It's the principle though —" Bernice began.

"Why are we still talking about this?" Sadie asked loudly. "I don't think what she did was wrong."

"But the food wasn't hers to give away," Bernice protested.

"She's part of the church same as everyone else here. Anyone other than Bernice have a problem with what Agnes did?" Sadie scanned the crowd.

"The person who donated the food intended the money to go to the church," Bernice said.

"What did you give him?" Sadie asked.

"Two loaves of brown bread, a tub of homemade beans, a frozen casserole, and a jug of milk from the fridge," Agnes replied.

"The brown bread is mine and I'm not concerned it went to him instead of earning some money," Sadie said. "Who donated the beans and casserole?"

"The beans were mine," Joyce piped up. "If he liked them tell him I'll give him some more. Was it a large or small casserole?"

"Small," Agnes said. "In a foil container."

"That would make it Carol's" Joyce said. "She lost a son in Iraq so you know she isn't going to mind you feeding a hungry vet."

"But the milk —"

Sadie stomped her foot. "Bernice do you care that much about a jug of milk?"

Bernice stopped for a moment and looked at the assembled women. "No, I guess it doesn't matter that much. I just wish that Agnes had asked for permission before she gave away the food for the sale."

"That much I agree." Sadie turned to Agnes. "Let us know if he comes around again so we can see if there is anything else we can do to help him."

There was a general murmur of agreement which even Bernice participated in and gradually the women went back to getting ready for the church sale.

Proper 17 / Pentecost 15 / Ordinary Time 22
Luke 14:1, 7-14

Learning in Humility

Maddy grimaced as she hit the wrong notes. She kept playing the offering piece for Sunday but knew she had messed up the whole middle section again. She had no problem with the start and the end but the change in key and tempo part way through was frustrating her despite hours of practice.

She pushed aside the music, switched the stops on the organ, and began her favorite hymn from memory. The music reverberated in the empty church and her spirit began to soar. She prayed with every note and offered praise with every measure. Maddy let the music lift her to heaven and as she came to the end allowed the echo of the final notes to bring her back to earth.

The sound of a single person clapping filled the sanctuary. Maddy turned to see a small grey haired man sitting in the very back seat. He was dressed as most men of his generation with a white shirt and tie. His hair was unkempt and he had a moustache which desperately needed to be shaped and trimmed. He stood and limped his way to the front of the church.

"My apologies if I startled you." The man stopped and gave her a toothy smile. "I heard you playing as I walked past. The door was open and I just couldn't help myself and slipped into the back. You have a wonderful talent."

"Thank you," Maddy blushed, "I didn't know that there was anyone here."

"No, thank *you*. It was a treat to hear such a magnificent composition being played with such enthusiasm and energy." He bowed. "I used to play in my small country church when I was a younger man and remember that hymn requires a deft touch."

Maddy looked down at the keyboard. "This is a wonderful instrument to play and sometimes I just lose myself in the music."

"Ah, would you mind if an old man took a closer look?" He paused at the stairs leading up to the organ until she nodded. He slowly and carefully made his way up. Even though it was only a few steps, he was out of breath when he reached her. He sat in one of the choir seats near the organ bench and squinted as he examined the instrument.

"Ah, this has been well cared for in its life. Would you mind playing a bit more? What about that piece open before you?"

Maddy hesitated as she looked at the music that had frustrated her all week. She glanced back at the old man in his wrinkled clothes and realized that if he had assumed the hymn was difficult that he'd have no idea how complicated this offertory piece was. She smiled and began to play. She let the music wash over her and watched the man out of the corner of her eye. He sat beaming at her. She felt a deep pride as she played and didn't wince as she came to the part she struggled with even though she floundered in that section.

She turned after she was finished. "I'm still polishing it."

He nodded. "It is a difficult piece but does showcase both your talent and this wonderful organ. May I?"

She stepped aside and let him sit down. He squinted at the music and nodded to himself. His hands touched the keys and he began to play. Maddy stood open-mouthed as she watched the organ come alive underneath his fingers. She had never heard angels sing but assumed they would sound like the music he was creating as his fingers danced over the keys and his feet flew on the pedals. He finished and looked up at her with the same smile he had when complimenting her music.

Her eyes were wide. "I thought you said you used to play in your country church?"

"That was how I fell in love with music. For years I toured as a concert pianist but my first love has always been the organ." He pointed toward the notes of the offertory. "I think this is where you start to have problems, yes?"

Mandy looked at the old man with different eyes and saw the years on his face not as marks of his incompetence but signs of the years of wisdom and experience he had accumulated. She nodded.

"I've run into similar problems in different pieces," he said. "Would you mind if I offered some suggestions?"

Maddy shook her head, sat down on the bench next to him, and with an open heart and mind began to learn from someone who wished her talent and skill to increase and grow.

Proper 18 / Pentecost 16 / Ordinary Time 23
Luke 14:25-33

First Things First

Donna scrunched up her face as she examined her calendar. "I'm not sure I can make it."

"You have to be there." Jolene put her hands on her hips, "It's the most important day of my life. You just can't miss it!"

"You are going shopping for an outfit to wear on your birthday. It is not like you are getting married."

"Who knows? Maybe Mr. Right will be there." Jolene swept a hand down her body. "If I don't look amazing then he might fall in love with someone else."

Donna cocked her head to one side. "Do you realize how many things are wrong with that statement?"

Jolene waved at the air. "What is so important that you can't come shopping with your best friend?"

"There's a youth rally at the church. I promised to help in the kitchen and to sing with the choir."

"So what?" Jolene said. "Can't you cancel?"

"The rally is a pretty big thing."

"Bigger than our friendship? Come on, help me out in my time of need."

Donna tapped at the screen of her phone. "I guess."

"That's great." Jolene pushed her toward the door. "See you later."

Donna stood in the hallway as the door to Jolene's room slammed shut. She slowly walked toward her residence room wondering if there was some way she could do the baking early and arrive at the youth rally late in order to keep Jolene happy.

Her phone beeped and she looked down at a text message from the worship leader for the rally linking to the music they would be singing and thanking her for adding her voice to the choir. Donna sighed loudly.

"Wow, someone is stressed." Hailey rolled her wheelchair to her doorway.

Donna smiled. "Just some scheduling problems. You know what it's like."

"Like when you tried to do everything at the end of last term? How many things were you doing at the same time as the prayer service for the disaster in Africa?"

Donna tapped her chin. "I was looking after the music and keeping Jolene happy after her breakup."

Hailey narrowed her eyes. "As well as trying to tutor Stephanie, keep Kimmie from calling her ex, and about a dozen other things."

Donna shrugged. "They needed my help."

"You were miserable that whole night. Some people came but they didn't stay when they saw you running around. Plus Jolene bawled her eyes out all night, Stephanie ended up leaving, Kimmie talked to her ex for over and hour and what else?"

"Okay so maybe the night didn't go well." Donna looked down at her phone. "I'm keeping stuff in my calendar this year so I'm better organized."

"So how's that going for you?"

Donna sighed. "Not so well. There's so much I want to do."

Hailey took Donna's hand. "Everyone knows you have a good Christian heart."

"Thanks."

Hailey squeezed her hand. "So why aren't you using it more?"

"Huh?" Donna frowned. "I'm helping as many people as I can."

"Really? From where I'm sitting you're just running from one thing to another and doing all of it poorly." Hailey looked her in the eye. "You have already promised to do other things the night of the rally, haven't you?"

Donna pulled her hand back. "I thought you were my friend."

"I am. You need to decide what is important and stick to it. Otherwise you are no good to the people around you or to God." Hailey rolled back into her room.

Donna opened her mouth to say something but closed it. She went to her room and flopped on the bed. Hailey didn't understand. There were so many people counting on Donna and she knew there had to be a way to help them all. Her phone beeped again and she looked at the text from the rally organizers asking her to confirm that she was helping with refreshments that night. Donna started to reply when she noticed that she was supposed to be in the kitchen at the same time Jolene expected her to be shopping.

Donna looked at the calendar for a long time. She tried to figure out a way around it but kept hearing Hailey's words about doing everything poorly when she tried to do please everyone. There was no way she could do all the things she wanted to do that night. Donna closed her eyes and prayed for wisdom and strength.

When she finished she knew what she had to do. She took a deep breath and headed down to see Jolene and tell her that she wasn't able to go shopping. Donna was already committed to something important that night and there was no way she was going to let anything interfere with those plans.

Proper 19 / Pentecost 17 / Ordinary Time 24
Luke 15:1-10

Divine Persistence

Hester was not a good person. She lied, cheated, and did whatever she wanted to do. She knew her actions hurt others and hurt herself on more than one occasion but she didn't care. Hester was angry at life and angry at God.

Hester grew up in a religious household with the finest role models imaginable. Her parents were generous and kind, prayed and read the scriptures each day, and attended church regularly. They loved their little girl and she loved them. They had their difficult days as any family does but Hester flourished because of her parent's love.

She grew from a bright and inquisitive girl to a young woman who could do whatever she put her mind to doing. She approached each day with enthusiasm and optimism. Everyone assumed that Hester would do great things in her life. Then tragedy struck. Her parents were killed by a drunk driver on their way home from choir practice.

The senseless accident devastated Hester. At the funeral, she sat stone faced while people expressed their condolences and the pastor tried to speak words of comfort. She became more and more bitter over what had happened as the weeks passed. Her parents were good people who did the right things and Hester was furious at God for letting them die in an accident. She decided that if God was going to let bad things happen that she was going to not care about God or what God wanted for her life.

Hester went to live with her aunt who was patient and loving with the hurting young woman. Hester, though, would have none of it. She knew her aunt was trying to help but Hester didn't care. She hated seeing people happy and pushed away those closest to her. She kept all of her hurt and anger inside of herself and refused to talk to her aunt, to the pastor, or to the counselors her aunt took her to see.

One day as they drove home from yet another appointment where Hester had refused to speak to a counselor, Hester turned to her aunt. "You should give up on me."

Her aunt shook her head, "Never."

Hester snorted, "I'll never be the wonderful young woman you want me to be."

"I will never give up on you." Her aunt's voice was firm and clear.

"You're crazy."

"No," her aunt looked over. "I love you."

Hester took that exchange as a challenge. When her aunt prayed Hester scoffed. When her aunt was nice Hester was mean. When her aunt made her go to church, Hester sat with her arms folded and either sighed or snorted through the service. She broke curfew repeatedly and skipped school on a regular basis. She was as selfish, spiteful, and untrustworthy as she could be.

One night as she crept into the house after sneaking out she heard her aunt praying "Lord, give me your strength and your grace to love Hester as you love her."

Something inside Hester snapped at that moment and all the rage, anger, and hurt came spilling out.

"God's doesn't love me," Hester screamed. "If he did then he wouldn't have taken my parents from me."

Her aunt came over and wrapped Hester in her arms. "What happened to your parents does not change the fact that God loves you."

Tears ran down Hester's face as great sobs wracked her body. "God doesn't care about me."

"Yes, he does," her aunt said. "I know that."

"How can you know that?" Hester demanded. "How can you possibly know that God cares about me? Especially after all I have done since my parents died?"

"God doesn't love you because you are good. God loves you because that is who God is."

"You can't know that!" Hester sobbed.

Her aunt's voice was certain and firm. "I know that as well as I know anything else in this world."

Hester's tears slowed and her voice grew calmer. "How?"

"Because I love you." Her aunt stroked her hair. "And I am not as patient, as caring, and as forgiving as God. Which means that God loves you even more that I do."

"I am not a very good person. I've done some bad things since the accident." Hester snuggled into her aunt's arms. "Why don't you give up on me?"

"I've already answered that, child." Her aunt kissed her forehead, "I love you."

Hester allowed herself to be held and in that moment there was a spark of peace which settled into her heart. Her aunt smiled and quietly thanked God for letting the grace of heaven touch their lives that night.

Proper 20 / Pentecost 18 / Ordinary Time 25
Luke 16:1-13

Who Do You Serve?

"It doesn't matter."

That's what Judy told herself when she put the dollar bill into the pocket of her shirt. The cash in the register at the grocery store was one dollar over and the rule was that they could not leave until the amount was reconciled. She had counted three times and tried to figure out why she had more money than she was supposed to but couldn't make it work. The night shift had already started and she had school the next morning. So she simply took the extra dollar. She turned in her tray and nodded to the person behind the security wicket.

She never thought about the dollar until she went to sign in the next day and discovered a note asking her to see the manager on duty. The money came to mind and her hand reached into her pocket and touched the bill. She remembered how everyone had difficulty getting their cash to reconcile the night before. Had someone put it there in her drawer to test for her honesty? Had she failed by simply pocketing the money?

Judy felt her skin grow warm as she walked up the stairs to the office. She knocked on the door and opened it. Mrs Jorgen' eyes seemed to see through Judy as she motioned her to sit down.

"Judy, how long have you been here at the store?"

Judy found it hard to swallow. She was being dismissed. "Two years now."

Mrs. Jorgen's eyes flicked to her computer. "Good reports from your supervisors I see."

Judy's mouth was dry and her tongue thick. Images of the years she spent here started rushing through her head. She liked this job. She liked the people and hours. "I've liked working here."

"That's nice." Mrs. Jorgen tapped on the keyboard and clicked the mouse. "You sometimes work the night shift, don't you?"

Judy nodded.

Mrs. Jorgen's finger touched the screen as she read something. "You worked that shift last night, didn't you?"

Judy shifted in her chair. The store had a very strict no tolerance policy for theft. The year she was hired two of the teens who worked on the front registers had been let go for taking chocolate bars without paying for them. She should never have pocketed that dollar. It was a test and she failed.

Judy looked down at the floor. "I did."

"Is something the matter?"

The older woman was no longer looking at the computer in front of her but at the Judy. "Do you have something you want to say to me?"

Judy's mind kicked into overdrive. Was it really that important? After all it was only a single. The store sold tens of thousands of dollars in merchandise each day. What did they care about a dollar from one cash register? Besides the tape said that she turned in the right amount of money. Who was to say she had done anything wrong?

Judy found it difficult to swallow. She imagined her parents looking on with disapproval at what she had done. She remembered the sermon from church last Sunday when Pastor Vernon told everyone how hard it was to do the right thing and how important small things were in a life of faith. The dollar bill was small but the fact was that she took something that didn't belong to her was huge. She took a deep breath and decided what she needed to do.

"Last night my cash drawer was over and I couldn't get it to balance." Judy took the dollar out of her pocket. "It was late and I'd always been told that we're not allowed to leave until we got the drawers to reconcile to the output from the register. I'm sorry."

"Why are you telling me all of this?" Mrs. Jorgen picked up the bill in her hand. "You could have just kept quiet and no one would have ever known."

Judy looked at the floor. "I would have known. Keeping something that belongs to another person is wrong no matter how small the amount is."

Mrs. Jorgen turned the note over in her hand. She opened her desk drawer, pulled out a form and slid it toward Judy. "Fill this out."

Judy looked down and her eyes went wide. The form was to submit a cash overage when the balance would not reconcile. Mrs. Jorgen's signature was already at the bottom as store manager.

"You need to fill that out before your shift starts." Mrs. Jorgen's eyes flicked to the clock on the wall. "I'm glad you like working here because you are a pleasure to have on staff."

"Thank you." Judy felt a burden lift off her shoulders as she headed out into the hallway. She went to her shift aware that she had learned something very important — the power of mercy and the importance of being faithful in all things.

Proper 21 / Pentecost 19 / Ordinary Time 26
Luke 16:19-31

No Greater Witness

Ida worked her way through the crowds of people gathered for fellowship time. She nodded to a couple of neighbors and waved to an old friend across the hall. The crush was a little lighter in front of the coffee and tea urns so she made her way over there.

"I think some tea, please." Ida picked up an empty cup and handed it to Laura. "I love seeing the church filled with so many people."

"It's been a great anniversary for the congregation that's for certain." Laura smiled as she poured. "Wasn't it wonderful to hear Pastor Kevin speak again?"

"My Charlie, God rest his soul, always thought Pastor Kevin was the best preacher to ever step into a pulpit." Ida sipped her tea and nodded her thanks. "I think he may be right. No one can preach an inspirational sermon like Pastor Kevin. I could feel the Holy Spirit at work when he spoke."

Ida turned her attention back to the crowd. There were so many faces she hadn't seen in years. She noticed the Andersons who used to live down the street. Hazel and George looked like they always had but it took her a moment to realize that the young man standing with them was their son, Bruce. He had gone to youth group with her Stephen. Ida turned away. The thought of Stephen made her heart ache. She wished he would have come with her this morning. Ida pretended not to see Hazel and George wave. She couldn't bear to face them.

She caught sight of Pastor Kevin holding a plate of sandwiches and heading toward an empty table. Ida set her sights on him and didn't allow anything to stop her from getting there. He placed his food next to the Bible and papers on the table and greeted her warmly.

"Pastor Kevin." She gave him a big hug, "Thank you so much for preaching at our service this morning."

"Ida, it's wonderful to see you." He returned the hug. "What a fabulous anniversary celebration for the congregation."

Ida looked behind him. "Is Mary not with you this morning?"

"She wasn't able to be here," Pastor Kevin said. "Our daughter is expecting her first child so Mary went to help out."

"Well do give her my best when you see her."

"I certainly will." Pastor Kevin took her hand. "I was so sorry to hear about Charlie. Even after his long illness it still must be hard."

"Thank you, it is. I still miss him." Ida wiped one of her eyes with a tissue. "Your sympathy card was a great comfort."

"I'm glad."

Ida looked at the papers on the table. "Do you still send out copies of your sermons?"

"Certainly, I have copies for those who are interested. Do you want one?"

"I do." She leaned closer and her voice dropped to a whisper. "Stephen has lost his faith and I think your words might help him find his way back to God."

Pastor Kevin reached over and plucked out a few of the papers. "I'm not sure if this will help but you're welcome to it."

"Your words this morning were so moving." Ida's brow furrowed. "How can you have any doubts that they will help Stephen return to church?"

"I assume you are still living the good Christian life you have always lived. Still volunteering with the clothing bank and going to Bible study?"

Ida nodded.

"Then you are giving him a good witness through your life." Pastor Kevin gestured at the people in the room. "I know the congregation here is a good example of a faithful church and I have never met a mind as sharp as Pastor Fred's, so if Stephen had any questions that needed to be answered I'm sure they would be answered here."

Ida sighed. "I just wish there was more that I could do to get him find his faith again."

"Keep doing everything you are doing. Pray for him. Keep showing him your Christian example and keep inviting him. Other than that there's not much more you can do," Pastor Kevin said. "You raised him well and he knows where he'll always be welcome. Ultimately it's his choice as an adult what to do about his faith."

Ida nodded and seeing the growing number of people waiting to talk to Pastor Kevin she thanked him one more time, picked up her tea, and headed back into the crowd. She was still sad about Stephen not being with her but Pastor Kevin's words seemed to soothe some of the ache she felt. She saw the Andersons starting to move toward the door and headed for them with determination. She wasn't going to miss a chance to say hello and catch up.

Proper 22 / Pentecost 20 / Ordinary Time 27
Luke 17:5-10

Faithful Servants

Amy slumped over in her chair and put her hands in her hair. "I'm going to quit choir."

"Why?" John turned down the pan on the stove and glanced over at the recipe he was following without looking at his daughter. "I thought you loved singing in church."

"I do. I love singing but I'm not sure that the youth choir is the place for me to do that."

"Have you had a fight with Kim again?" John reached over the stove and picked out some spices.

Amy shook her head and then realized her father wasn't looking at her. "No. We're getting along fine."

"Set the table, will you?"

Amy went over to the drawers and started to pull out cutlery. "Just the two of us, or will Mom make it home for supper?"

"She has a late appointment but might get here for dessert so set her a place." John added some more oil to the pan. "Is Judy not picking pieces that you like to sing? I thought you loved the variety and being able to learn all sorts of different music."

"No, it has nothing to do with the music and you know that Judy is great."

John measured out the ingredients and added them to the simmering meat. "Then why would you leave choir?"

"Just because."

John stopped what he was doing and looked over at his daughter. "Not good enough."

Amy shifted in her chair a few times. "They don't appreciate me."

"What do you mean?"

"Well, I go to choir every practice and take the time to make sure I know the words and everything and no one really notices me."

"Pastor Carl always speaks highly of the choirs in our church so I know he appreciates the music ministry." John pulled out some potatoes and started to chop them into fine pieces. "Wait a moment. Doesn't Judy thank you by name in the annual choir report?"

Amy rolled her eyes. "She mentions everyone."

John added the potatoes to the pan and turned up the heat. "So doesn't everyone deserve a mention? Are you the only one who learns the words and goes to practice?"

Amy scowled. "You know what I mean, Dad."

"No, I don't." John got out a wooden spoon and stirred the sizzling ingredients in the pan. "Explain it to me."

"It's just that no one appreciates the time and effort I take in the choir." Amy shrugged. "I thought you were supposed to thank people when they do things for you."

"You are."

"People don't seem to appreciate my work practicing so I'm not going to do it anymore." Amy folded her arms.

"So you sing in church to be thanked?"

"No." Amy frowned. "That just makes me sound shallow."

"You're not shallow but your words might be." John kept stirring. "Why do you sing in church?"

"It's part of our worship service."

John nodded. "Exactly and you have the gift of music. So why should you not be expected to share it with everyone else?"

"So you're saying that when we can do something we should do it," Amy said. "Whether or not anyone thanks us?"

John started to dish out the finished meal. "Pretty much."

"That doesn't seem fair to me." Amy put the full plates on the table. "People should do things because they want to do them."

John walked over to his chair and kissed his daughter on the forehead. "If that was the way things were then you would go hungry, my dear."

Amy opened her mouth to say something but closed it instead. Her eyes wandered over to the kitchen and then back to the table where her father was waiting for them to say grace.

"You know I appreciate you making supper, don't you Dad? Your cooking is so much better than Mom's."

"That is nice to hear," John said. "But it doesn't change the fact of why I cook supper for you and do all the other things I do. I do them because I can and they are part of what I am expected to do as a member of this family. That's no different than the obligation you have as member of God's household."

Amy slowly nodded and bowed her head as John gave thanks for the meal. When she opened her eyes she breathed in the wonderful smell of the stir fry.

"I think maybe I should keep singing in the church choir."

John smiled. "I'm glad because you really do have a lovely voice."

Amy blushed and the two of them proceeded to eat the meal before them.

Proper 23 / Pentecost 21 / Ordinary Time 28
Luke 17:11-19

Thankful Harvest

There once was a man who purchased a barren field. He wanted there to be beauty and life in the field so he spread seeds upon the ground. He gently covered them with a layer of soil to protect them from the storms that blew through and went away until the season of growth arrived.

That season came when the sun warmed the ground and the gentle rains fell on the earth. With warmth and wetness the seeds sprouted. Nourished by the soil around them they began to grow into the beautiful plants they were meant to be. They grew from mere shoots into plants that reached toward the sky and spread out their leaves. Then each one of the plants budded and formed colorful flowers and the field was beautiful and wonderful to behold. Except for one corner where ten seeds had failed to grow.

For in that corner of the field a tree branch had blown down in a windstorm before the seeds sprouted. Hidden from the warmth of the sun and covered so the rain could not reach them, the ten seeds never reached their potential. They sat under the cold ground. They waited for someone to release them from their situation so they could rise up and flourish. They watched as the other seeds blossomed, grew, and unfolded their flowers and wished they could do the same. But with no sunlight and no rain they could not grow and they did not grow.

One day in the season of growth, the owner came walking through the field admiring the flowers in all of their colors and sizes. He noticed the fallen branch and heard the seeds lamenting that they were trapped and needed someone to save them. He picked up the branch and leaned down to the ground and whispered to the ten seeds "grow as you were meant to grow."

When morning came and the sun touched the ground that had been hidden the seeds warmed and began to change. When the rains came and watered the soil they sprouted and grew. The seeds joyfully shot to the surface and began to reach to the sky. They produced leaves which allowed them to unfold their flowers, as colorful and lovely as any of the other flowers in the field. Nine of them reached for the warmth of the sun and eagerly embraced the rain and rejoiced that nothing held them back from being like every other flower in the field. Nine grew that way but one responded a different way.

One seed sprouted and grew leaves and unfolded a beautiful flower. It reached for the sun and embraced the rain as did the nine other seeds that had been released by the owner of the field. Except this seed which grew into a flower did not merely revel in the field and the growth, did not simply enjoy the season where the sun was warm and the rain was refreshing. That seed which grew into a plant thought of the owner and the words which had been spoken to it.

That one plant spent time thinking about what it was meant to do and how it was meant to grow. It thought of the owner planting all of the seeds and knew that it was intended to grow and blossom. Yet it also realized that it was meant to produce beauty in gratitude to the owner. That plant did something different than the nine who were like all of the other seeds in the field who grew leaves and flowers. It thought of the owner as it stretched to the sky.

When the owner walked through the field the next time he looked at all of the wonderful flowers and came to the place where the seeds had been trapped under the branch. He looked at the nine and saw their beautiful flowers and leaves. Then he saw the one grateful plant and saw its flowers and leaves and what else it had produced. That one plant had seeds waiting for the owner to collect.

With a gentle touch the owner gathered the offered seeds and smiled at the one plant. "Your thankfulness will produce a bounty" the owner whispered. The other plants did not understand what was happening. Their flowers were just as lovely and their leaves just as wide as that one plant. What could the owner mean?

The growing season ended and the sun was not as warm as before and the rain no longer helped the plants to grow. As their flowers fell and their leaves started to wither, the plants began to return to the earth, assuming that they had seen and done all that was intended. The one grateful plant, though, knew better. It knew that when the owner returned before the next season of growth to prepare the field, some of its seeds would be part of what the owner used to bring new life to the earth.

Proper 24 / Pentecost 22 / Ordinary Time 29
Luke 18:1-8

Powerful Persistence

"Lisa has fallen out of bed again!"
Lisa ignored the taunt as she knelt beside her bunk and bowed her head. Even though she was aware that everyone in the room was watching her, she closed her eyes. She tried to focus on what she knew she was supposed to do.

She prayed for the counselors who were working at the summer camp. She prayed for her parents and family. She prayed for everyone else and everything else she could think of before taking a deep breath. She didn't know why she was supposed to do this but she knew it was important. She began praying by name for the girls who were making fun of her. The teasing died down as she crawled under the covers and tried not to cry. After a few moment the conversation in the room turned away from her and focused on other things.

Stacy hung down from the top bunk and whispered. "Why do you do that?"

Lisa wondered what other way she had offended this group of girls. "Do what?"

"Pray. Why not just forget about it here?" Stacy scowled. "They will keep teasing you as long as you do."

"I always pray before going to bed," Lisa said. "I always have and always will."

"You're stupid." Stacy shook her head. "They would leave you alone if you just stopped."

Lisa sighed. "I know."

The next morning at breakfast Marcie smiled at her innocently. "Lisa, I was wondering something."

Lisa's stomach knotted as she looked up from her food. "What's that?"

"How did you get into our cabin?" Marcie twirled her hair around her finger.

Lisa shrugged her shoulders. "I think they randomly assign them."

"No, I meant how did a baby like you get into our cabin?" Marcie tittered.

"I'm only a couple of months younger than you, Marcie."

"Oh, you keep falling out of bed every night." The smile turned into a sarcastic grin. "I thought you were much, much younger."

The other girls around the table giggled.

Lisa put her elbows on the table and stared at Marcie. She ignored Stacy's head shaking back and forth urging her to just be quiet. "You know very well that I am not falling out of bed, Marcie. I'm praying because I'm a Christian and that is what we do."

Marcie put her elbows on the table and glared back. "What is so important that you need to talk to God all the time?"

"I believe that is what Jesus wants us to do. To pray for things that are wrong to make them right." She held Marcie's gaze. "No matter what people think."

"Oh, so you think you're better than all of us then?"

"No. I don't."

"So what is so important that you have to pray about it each night?"

"I pray for my family and friends, the counselors who are working with us at camp, and places in the world where things are not right." Lisa took a deep breath. "And I pray for all of you."

"Do you think that God might be able to stop us from teasing you? Do I need to watch out?" Marcie covered her head for a moment and then looked around. "Hey, no lightning bolts. I guess God doesn't care about your prayers."

The other girls giggled.

"Yes, I do pray that the teasing will stop but that is not all I pray about when I think of you." Lisa looked Marcie in the eyes. "I also pray that your Mom will find a job and your brother might come home safely from overseas."

The bell chimed and the counselors arrived to tell everyone it was time to go onto the next activity.

That night before bed Lisa knelt to pray.

"Lisa has fallen out of bed again." Ava called out. The others girls picked up the chant.

Ava went over and shook Marcie. "Marcie did you not hear? We said that Lisa has fallen out of her bed."

Marcie rolled over and glared at her. "She didn't fall out of bed. She's praying. That's what she does before bed."

"But isn't it because she is a baby? Isn't she just a little baby who falls out of bed?" Ava grinned widely and looked around the room. The other girls went silent and her eyes came back to Marcie's unsmiling face.

"Grow up, Ava. Some people pray. I think it's stupid but if she wants to do it what do I care?" Marcie rolled back over.

Ava slunk back to her bed. Lisa simply closed her eyes and began to pray.

Proper 25 / Pentecost 23 / Ordinary Time 30
Luke 18:9-14

The Humble Soul

Ike whistled as he came through the office doors. He stuffed his gloves and hat into his pocket and hung his coat on the hook. He turned and grinned at Heather.

"Good morning."

Heather looked up from her computer and smiled. "You're in a good mood for a Monday morning."

"Why shouldn't I be?" Ike picked up the mail from the edge of the desk. "Things are going well for me."

"You have some messages." Heather looked at her watch. "You want them in fifteen minutes like normal?"

Ike shook his head. "No, today I don't think I need that time. Just give me a couple of minutes to settle in."

"Really?" Heather said. "For the past three years you've taken fifteen minutes for prayer at the start of each day. What's different now?"

"Everything is going perfectly. My marriage is good, kids are happy, work is under control. I had a wonderful weekend." Ike's grin grew wider. "I even had a great night's sleep. I'm ready to get to work."

"You've always said to me that starting the morning with prayer gets you grounded and ready for the work ahead." Heather frowned. "Looking at these messages I think it is going to be a long day."

"God has richly blessed me so I can handle it." Ike headed into his office. "No need to bother God when I have things under control."

Ike wasn't smiling on Friday morning when he came through the door. He picked up the mail from the desk and nodded at Heather.

"Meetings not go well last night?" she asked.

"They went fine. The reports should be in place well before the deadlines." He reached out for his messages and after looking at them for a moment let out a loud sigh. "I'll start working through the backlog. This has been one busy, chaotic week."

"Actually I think this week was a bit lighter for us than previous weeks have been."

"All I know is that I am beat." Ike slumped down in the chair next to her desk. "The past few days have just about wiped me out. I wonder if maybe I've picked up a bug."

"You seem as healthy as ever." Heather looked him in the eyes. "Your problem is that you stopped taking the time for prayer."

Ike shook his head. "I'm still praying."

"What are you praying about?"

"I'm thankful for all of my blessings and all the great things I am able to do." Ike waved his hands at the office. "I may forget it on occasion but this really is my dream position. The work we do here is important and I know we're making a difference."

Heather narrowed her eyes. "What were you praying about when we started three years ago?"

Ike scratched his head. "I mostly asked God for help. I'd go through the past day and pray for forgiveness and the ability and wisdom to do a better job than I'd done. Then I would pray for the grace to make it through the day before me."

"So why the change?"

"I know what I am doing now." Ike looked at the photographs and awards on the walls. "We have some successes behind us. Let's face it when we started we had no idea what we were up against."

Heather chuckled. "Yeah, I remember those days."

"Now I know I can handle whatever comes through those doors." Ike sighed. "Yet I kind of miss those days. The excitement and the rush of helping and learning."

"So what's changed?"

Ike frowned. "I told you. I know what I'm doing now."

"Really? Then why do you feel like a failure this morning?"

He stared at her for a moment. "How did you know?"

"We've been working together long enough for me to know when you're down." Heather took a breath. "Hopefully we are good enough colleagues for me to be honest with you."

Ike nodded.

"You need to start praying again like you did before." Heather pointed to the clock. "Don't shortchange God or yourself. Take the time you need each day."

Ike said nothing for a few moments and then sighed very loudly. "I've gotten a bit full of myself lately, haven't I?"

"Honestly?" Heather locked eyes with him. "Yes, you have."

He looked away for a moment. "I'm sorry."

"I'm not the one you need to talk to." She pointed up. "You need to get your prayer life in order."

"I agree. Please give me fifteen minutes before you pass along my messages." Ike got up from the chair. "Heather?"

"Yes?"

"Thank you for being such a good friend."

Heather smiled. "Remember me when you're praying."

Ike smiled back and headed into his office to put his life back on the right path.

Proper 26 / Pentecost 24 / Ordinary Time 31
Luke 19:1-10

Who Is Worthy?

Jane stood at the door of the church and read the sign another time. Were they really serious about "Everyone Welcome"? If she went through these doors would they make a place for her? Was she worthy to be part of a church?

She heard the sounds of talking inside grow louder and stepped back onto the sidewalk. A man and a woman came out of the church and smiled at her. Jane smiled back hesitantly.

"The Sunday service starts in a half hour," the woman said to her. "Are you coming in?"

Jane shook her head before continuing down the street. "Just passing by."

She heard the couple talking behind her. Did they know the type of person she was and what she'd done in her life? Were they thankful that she was leaving and not going into their church? Her heart sank. Would there ever be a time when she was able to go in and hear about Jesus?

Jane passed by the church later that week. She stopped and listened to the choir practicing and enjoyed the wonderful music. She sang softly with them until she realized she wasn't alone. The same woman from Sunday was standing behind her.

"You have a lovely voice," the woman said.

Jane felt her face grow warm. "It's nothing special."

"No, trust me I hear a lot of singers," the woman said. "You have a gift for music. Have you ever sung in a choir before?"

Jane shook her head. "No, I just mess around. I've never been part of a group."

The woman smiled. "We're always looking for new members for our community choir. You should join us one night."

Jane's heart began to race. "I really couldn't."

"Why not?"

"I'm on my way somewhere. Bye." Jane headed down the sidewalk. She slowed her pace when she heard the woman go into the church. Jane looked back and whispered. "Church isn't for people like me."

Jane stared at the sign from across the road. She watched the people talking and laughing and noticed the woman who had spoken to her heading into the church. All the people seemed to know each other and were so happy. She felt her chest ache. She wanted so much to go through the doors and share in that happiness. She wished she could go inside. She longed to have what they took for granted in their lives. She wanted to smile, to laugh, and to be part of something important.

"You know you're welcome to come to the church."

Jane turned to see the man who had come out with the woman last Sunday. She lowered her head and started away. "No, not today I think."

"Then when?" the man asked.

Jane stopped in her tracks. "What?"

"I saw you here last Sunday. Linda said you were listening to choir practice when they met during the week and I'm around here enough to know you pass by here a lot. So when are you going to come in?"

Jane looked at the ground. "Church really isn't for me."

"I disagree. It is for you."

Jane shook her head. "You don't know anything about me."

"And you don't know anything about me, do you?"

Jane looked up at him. "No, I don't."

"Then you don't know what I have done in my life and I don't know what you have done in your life."

Jane nodded. "That's about right."

The man tapped his chin with his finger. "I do know something about you."

Jane shifted side to side. "How can you if you don't know me?'

"I know the Bible says you are a child of God," the man replied. "I also know that the forgiveness of Jesus is greater than whatever it is that's keeping you from coming into the church."

Jane frowned. "How can you know that?"

"Because I was a long time coming into the church and accepting God's grace." The man started across the street. "You are welcome among God's people because you are one of God's people."

Jane watched him go into the church and heard the bells start to ring. She found her feet starting toward the door. Her heart was racing as she crossed the street. She hesitated in front of the church. What if the man was wrong? What if she wasn't welcome and God wasn't interested in having her in church?

She started to back away when another thought pushed the doubts out of her head. What if he was right? What if the things happening inside weren't just for other people but were also for people like her? What if God wanted her to come inside? Jane found her hand back on the door and with all her courage she pulled and took a step forward in faith.

Proper 27 / Pentecost 25 / Ordinary Time 32
Luke 20:27-38

Honoring the Word

Pamela stood in front of her bedroom door with her mouth hanging open. Her beautiful room, which she kept neat and clean with everything in its place, was a disaster. There were old newspapers and magazines strewn all over the floor. There was a pile of empty plastic bottles over in the corner and some collapsed boxes on top of and underneath the bed.

She ran down the hallway to the stairs. "Mom! Come quick!"

"Pamela, I told you to go to your room." Her mother appeared at the bottom step. "Did you not hear me?"

"I heard you but —"

"No excuses," her mother said. "What you did was wrong and you need to take some time to think about it."

Pamela put her hands on her hips. "I didn't lie when I asked to go to the sleepover at Margie's."

"You neglected to tell me that Margie's parents were going to be away that night."

"You never asked me whether they would be there so I didn't actually lie to you," Pamela said. "There is a difference."

Her mother shook her head. "We're not going through this again. Go to your room."

Pamela stood her ground. "Besides it wasn't such a bad thing because it lets you forgive me and forgiveness is good. Jesus wants us to forgive, right?"

"Room." Her mother pointed. "Now."

"I can't." Pamela looked down the hallway. "I can't go into my room."

"What's the matter?"

"You won't believe it." Pamela started down the hallway. "You have to come and see my room."

"I've seen your room before and don't need to see it again." Her mother moved out of sight. "If you are not in your room in two minutes then you are grounded for a week."

Pamela walked down three steps so she could look into the living room where her Mother was sitting. "Mom! You're not listening to me."

"I heard you. You want me to see your room." Her mother looked up from her book. "I told you to go to your room. I'll be up to talk to you after you've had time to think."

"You don't understand!" Pamela said. "Something terrible has happened!"

"Oh?" Her mother tilted her head to one side. "What's happened?"

"My room is a mess!"

Her mother went back to reading. "Then use your time to clean it up."

"Mom, you don't understand. My room is a mess. Someone dumped paper, plastic, and cardboard all over the room." Pamela scowled. "I bet it was Ivan. He's such a brat. You need to punish him for messing up my room."

"Ivan didn't dump the recyclables all over your room," her mother said.

"How can you know that?"

"I know because I put those things in your room."

Pamela's eyes went wide. "Why?"

"Because I know that the environment is something important to you and I wanted to give you lots of opportunity to recycle."

"But those things were already sorted and in recycling bags!"

"I know." Her mother looked her in the eyes. "I thought if you had a chance to recycle them again it would be that much better than just sorting them once. If it helped the planet to recycle them once then it must be twice as good to recycle them a second time."

"Mom, recycling doesn't work that way! You don't make things better for the earth by making a mess of items already sorted and then cleaning them up again." Pamela stopped and thought for a moment. "You know that already, don't you?"

"Really? Why do you think that?"

Pamela took a step back up the stairs. "You wanted me to understand that just because I can argue a point doesn't make it right or good."

"Actually I wanted you to see that twisting something good, like forgiveness, to serve your selfish need is wrong but what you are saying is a good lesson as well."

Pamela looked up the stairs. "So what am I supposed to do about my room?"

"The recycling bags are in the closet. Clean up your room and as you do think about what a waste of time it is." Her mother resumed reading. "Then I will come up and we will have a long talk about the waste of time it is to twist God's word in order to win an argument instead of learning from it."

Pamela opened her mouth to say something in reply but decided to keep quiet. She went back up the stairs and started to work. She had lots of time to consider what her mother had said as she refilled the recycling bags. She decided that from then on she would listen to the gospel instead of trying to get it to justify her point of view.

Proper 28 / Pentecost 26 / Ordinary Time 33
Luke 21:5-19

Considering Our Priorities

Charles slumped in his chair and sighed loudly.

Mary looked up. "There a problem, dear?"

Charles waved at the television. "Did you just see what I saw?"

"I wasn't paying attention." Mary held up a magazine opened on her lap. "Did something annoy you on television again?"

"Politicians. Another one arrested on suspicion of corruption." Charles shook his head. "I just don't know what is happening to our world."

"That is discouraging but I don't find it earth shattering. There always seems to be some bad apples taking advantage of the system." Mary looked over the top of her reading glasses at her husband. "Especially in some cities."

"I guess so." Charles narrowed his eyes. "The rest of them though can't seem to get anything done. They just speak and pose."

Mary took her reading glasses off and set them on the small table next to her chair. "The gridlock does seem to be more common than ever."

"Exactly." Charles sat up. "Do you know what happens when our government doesn't work the way it should work?"

"I suspect you are going to tell me."

"People get disheartened, that's what." Charles picked up the remote control. "I could turn to any news channel and the stories would be the same. Protest and rallies all the time. Our country is a mess."

Mary nodded. "Things are unsettled that's for sure."

"Worst of all is that nothing changes." Charles shook his head. "Our officials promise change and they may do a bit here or there but everything stays the same."

"That's kind of a pessimistic view, isn't it?"

"No, that's realistic." Charles sat forward in his chair. "If old folks like us are worried about what's happening in the world, what must it be like for our children or grandchildren? Everything is upside down all the time and there's violence and uncertainty. All the things we took for granted are gone."

"The kids seem to be doing okay."

"That's not the point. Think about all the things that they can't trust that we took for granted." He started counting on his fingers. "Government, banks, police, churches. When we were starting out you could trust them but now it seems like every week there is a scandal or controversy."

"I think you might be exaggerating, dear."

"Really? Name one profession that you trust absolutely like we used to when we were growing up."

Mary looked up at the ceiling for a moment her mouth moving soundlessly.

Charles clapped his hands. "See?"

She held up a finger. "Give me a moment."

Charles started tapping the armrest of his chair.

Mary glared at him and he stopped. Finally she spread her hands. "I can think of good people but no, things have changed in how we look at teachers, doctors, police, and clergy."

"So you agree with me then. Things have gotten much worse."

Mary shook her head. "No, I would argue that they've become different."

"I think that is a bit optimistic."

"So you prefer the days when people in authority could do anything they wanted to and no one questioned them?"

"Of course not." Charles frowned. "That's what led to abuse and the problems in the first place."

Mary tilted her head to one side. "You're not agreeing with me, are you?"

"No, I admit you're right that it is better not to put professions up on a pedestal." Charles pointed at the images on the television. "The protests and scandals are certainly not better."

Mary nodded. "Well, on that we agree."

Charles stroked his chin. "You know what I think is the biggest problem about the way things are in the world now?"

"What's that?"

"No-one trusts the institutions which were the cornerstones of this great land. The foundations on which we built prosperity no longer have our confidence. As a nation we have lost faith in the things which made this country great." Charles leaned back in his chair. "I'm afraid that means that we're on a dangerous path with no way back."

Mary looked at the images on the television for a moment and then looked into her husband's eyes. "As disciples of Jesus, isn't our faith supposed to be in God and not the human things around us?"

Charles stared at his wife for a moment and then nodded. She put her glasses back on and resumed reading her magazine. Charles sat back in his chair deep in thought. He was still thinking about the events of the land but now he was considering the place of grace and divine forgiveness in changing the world.

Christ the King (Proper 29) / Pentecost 27 / Ordinary Time 34
Luke 23:33-43

Heavenly Reception

Kate unloaded the tray of dirty dishes. "How many people do you think we've served this evening?"

Maria counted the pile of clean plates sitting on the counter. "Four left which means that we've sent out 76 dinners."

"Does that include take outs?"

Maria glanced at the containers on the shelf. "So we have served just over a hundred."

"Not a bad number given this time of year," Kate said.

"I agree." Maria looked out at the crowd of people in the church hall. "People seem quite happy."

"Roast beef is always a hit especially when it smells so wonderful." Kate took a deep breath. "Tell me that there is some left for the hungry workers."

"Have I ever let you down before?" Maria frowned. "Is that who I think it is in the corner?"

Kate turned. "Which corner?"

"Nearest the door."

"Is that Paula Freer?" Kate squinted. "I didn't recognize her with short hair. They must have made her cut it in prison."

"When did she get out?"

Kate shrugged. "Must have been recently. I haven't seen her around and she lives not far from me."

"She has some nerve showing her face in this church." Maria's hands went onto her hips.

Kate turned to look at her friend. "Why do you say that?"

"She stole from the grocery store where she was a cashier."

Kate frowned. "I thought the paper said she was convicted of passing bad checks."

"That's what they caught her for but you can bet she did more than that." Maria snorted. "If she did one bad thing you know she did more."

"Maybe."

"Trust me," Maria said. "I have it on good authority that's why they let her go down at the store."

Kate shrugged. "I still don't see why that means she can't be here at the supper."

Maria folded her arms. "She should be ashamed of herself."

"She never looked at me when I served her and I've known Paula since we were in high school," Kate said. "I'd say she is pretty ashamed."

"Not ashamed enough to stay away."

Kate's head tilted to the right. "Why should she stay away from a church supper?"

"Because she's a criminal that's why." Maria's eyes went over to the cash box near the door. "Someone should tell Linda so she can keep a closer eye on the money."

"Paula passed bad checks. It's not like she held up a bank."

"A criminal is a criminal."

Kate turned her attention back to Paula sitting in the corner by herself. "So that means a sinner is a sinner?"

Maria nodded enthusiastically. "Exactly."

"Then I guess you're right she shouldn't be here at this church supper." Kate looked back at her friend. "Someone should talk to her."

Maria's eyes went wide. "She's almost done. Maybe it would be safer to just say nothing."

"No, you're right. Someone needs to talk to her." Kate undid her apron and put it on the counter. "If I had known it was Paula I would have done this earlier."

Maria watched as Kate went over and sat down across from Paula. Paula started to get up but Kate touched her hand and she stayed at the table. Kate spoke for a moment and Paula nodded slowly. Paula wiped at her eyes as Kate headed back to the kitchen.

Maria handed the apron to Kate. "I guess you told her."

"Someone had to." Kate tied the apron in place. They both watched as Paula got out of her seat and headed out the door.

"So we have seen the last of her?" Maria asked.

"Maybe," Kate said. "I certainly hope not."

"What? I thought you told her to get out and stay away. Isn't that why she burst into tears?"

"Absolutely not." Kate looked back at the door Paula had just exited. "I told her she should come back to church and that she is always welcome to sit with me."

"But...but..." Maria sputtered. "She's a sinner. A criminal. Why would you do such a thing? How could you forgive her?"

Kate turned her attention to her friend. "Isn't that what Jesus did when he was on the cross?"

"That was different!"

"How?"

Maria opened and closed her mouth a few times. Finally she blurted out. "I don't want people like her coming to our church."

Kate locked eyes with Maria. "You think that is what Jesus would say to her?"

Maria looked away. "It's not going to be easy if she comes on Sunday."

"No, it isn't." Kate touched her friend's hand. "Which is why we should do everything we can to make sure she knows she is as welcome here as the rest of us sinners."

Maria looked at Kate and slowly nodded.

Reformation Day
John 8:31-36

Being Set Free

Frederick looked up at the door. He wiped his hands on his pants, raised a hand, and knocked firmly. The door opened and Mrs. Shaw smiled widely.
"Frederick, what a pleasant surprise. I wasn't expecting you until next week."
"Can I come in?"
Her brow furrowed. "Mr. Shaw is having a nap. How about you come back later?"
Frederick met her eyes. "Can I come in and speak with you?"
Mrs. Shaw stepped out of the way and gestured Frederick into the kitchen. He sat down in the place he usually sat and looked at Mr. Shaw's chair. Only yesterday they sat playing cards as Mr. Shaw told him stories about being in Korea and traveling around Asia as a young man. Just 24 hours ago Frederick had been free and untroubled.
"Do you want something to drink?"
Frederick couldn't take his eyes off the empty chair. "No, thank you."
Mrs. Shaw sat down beside him. "Want to tell me what the problem is?"
"I was here yesterday, you know."
"Yes, Mr. Shaw looks forward to the visits that you have with him." Mrs. Shaw frowned. "Did something happen while I went out to the store?"
Frederick looked at his feet. "Yes, Ma'am."

"Frederick you need to look at me. You didn't mention anything when I came back. You said everything went fine and he stayed in his chair."

Frederick nodded. "He did. He just told me stories about being in the army and when he went overseas."

Mrs. Shaw sighed. "I wish he would focus on happier memories. You shouldn't have to listen to those tales."

"I don't mind. I've heard most of them already and he gets so happy when he tells them." Frederick shrugged. "Sometimes he tells ones that I haven't heard before."

Mrs. Shaw reached out and patted his arm. "You're a good boy, Frederick."

"Not always, ma'am."

"Frederick, you know that Mr. Shaw isn't well and has episodes so I need you to be honest with me. Did he do something that hurt you?"

Frederick shook his head. "No, he did nothing wrong."

Mrs. Shaw frowned again. "I think you need to tell me what happened from the beginning."

Frederick's mouth became dry and it felt like the words were sticking in his throat but he forced them out. "We played some cards when I arrived like we usually do and he was asking me about the ball game last night."

Mrs. Shaw nodded. "I remember."

"Then Mr. Shaw started telling me about the World Series he went to see with his brother."

"I'd forgotten about that." Mrs. Shaw smiled. "I'm glad his disease has left him with some good memories. What happened then?"

"He told me a bit about how scared he was going overseas and some about his time doing patrols."

Mrs. Shaw sat forward. "I think that's about when I left."

"Yes, ma'am." Frederick found it hard to say the next few words but forced himself to keep talking. "Then he had one of his good times and called me Frederick and asked how my mother was keeping up with my father gone and all. That's when it happened."

"What?"

Frederick reached into his pocket. "He gave me some money to get something at the store."

"Frederick, is that what you're worried about?" Mrs. Shaw sat back in her chair. "I told you before that if he gives you money that's okay. You don't have to keep giving it back."

"No, ma'am. It's not okay." Frederick put the hundred dollar bill on the table between them.

Mrs. Shaw's eyes went wide.

"He gave me it in that way he used to tip waiters at the fancy restaurants and told me to just put it in my pocket. I meant to tell you but my Mom was waiting and I forgot." Frederick shifted in his seat. "I thought it was a one or a five at most."

"Thank you, Frederick. I think I need to find a better place to hide the grocery money." Mrs. Shaw looked at him. "You know most boys would simply have kept the money."

"I couldn't do that ma'am."

"No one would have known."

Frederick shook his head. "I had to come and tell you to be free from what happened and so you know I never meant to take it from him or from you."

Mrs. Shaw picked up the money from the table and put it in her purse. "I know, Frederick. You are a good Christian boy who has been such a blessing to us."

"Ma'am, doing what Jesus asks is just what you are supposed to do." Frederick looked up at her. "Can I still come back next week like usual?"

Mrs. Shaw got up from her seat and wrapped him in her arms. "I'm looking forward to it."

All Saints Day
Luke 6:20-31

Blessed Are You

"I'm a Christian," Stephanie said. The conversation in the group stopped. Four pairs of eyes turned to her. "I'm not going to be able to meet on Sunday morning because I go to church."

"What time?" Silvio asked.

"From ten until twelve." Stephanie waited as everyone looked at each other and said nothing.

Finally Ora shrugged. "I don't like getting out of bed before noon on weekends so that shouldn't be a problem."

"After twelve works better for me." Ted elbowed Ivan in the ribs. "Especially if we're still hung over from Saturday night."

Ivan pulled out his phone and tapped on it. "Works for me too. Say we meet around two in the afternoon?"

Everyone looked at Stephanie. "Sure, that's fine."

"Okay, we've settled when we can meet," Silvio said. "Does anyone know what we're supposed to do?"

Ted and Ivan shrugged. Ora opened her laptop and began typing. Stephanie pulled out a piece of paper. "The syllabus says we're supposed to do a ten minute animation on a topic of our choice."

"I don't think it will be that difficult to do," Silvio said.

Ora looked up from her computer and shook her head. "It has to be professional quality."

"Still not a problem. I have a friend who does graphic art for a living who can help us." Silvio winked. "If you know what I mean."

"Awesome!" Ivan and Ted high fived. "Easy A."

Stephanie cleared her throat. "I think that's a problem."

The room got very quiet again.

"Why?" Silvio asked.

"It's supposed to be our work." Stephanie held up the assignment. "That's what we are being graded on."

Silvio rolled his eyes. "Are you going to work in animation when you graduate?"

"I doubt it," Stephanie admitted.

Silvio folded his arms. "Then why do you care if we get some outside help?"

"Because it's wrong."

"Oh, come on." Silvio threw up his arms. "Everyone does it."

Stephanie shook her head. "That doesn't make it right."

"Guys, back me up." Silvio looked over at Ted and Ivan. "I need the mark to keep my scholarship."

"Hey less work means more party time." Ted stood next to Silvio. "I say we go the easy way."

"I'm swamped with my science courses as it is." Ora closed her laptop. "If Silvio has a friend who can free up some time for me, I'm all for it."

Stephanie narrowed her eyes. "Will this friend just help us or are you going to get him to do everything for us?"

"He will just help us to get the best grade. No worry, hassle, or fuss." Silvio smiled. "Isn't that what college is all about?"

Stephanie stood up. "I came here to learn."

"I came here to learn history not animation," Ivan said. "What is this friend going to want for doing this?"

"Shoot me the guidelines, Ora, and I'll text him and see." Silvio reached for his phone. "I'm sure his rates are reasonable."

"I can't be a part of this," Stephanie said.

Silvio walked over until he was face-to-face with her. "Listen miss holier-than-thou. If you go to the professor asking to change groups then she is going to want to know why. What are you going to say?"

Stephanie took a deep breath and refused to budge. "The truth."

Silvio's face went red and his fist started clenching and unclenching.

Ora cleared her throat. "I just realized I can't meet on Sunday afternoons. It will have to be in the morning."

Ted and Ivan looked at each other. "Yeah. We do our best work hung over so Sunday morning is the only time that makes sense for us."

"Sounds perfect to me." Silvio's fingers danced over his phone's keypad. "I just sent a note to the professor asking for her to find you a different group because you refuse to meet with us when we are available."

"You know I go to church."

Silvio shrugged and walked back to the others. "Yeah, I also let her know that you are upset with us as well because we won't use a friend of yours to do the work instead of doing it ourselves."

"But I'm the only one who doesn't want to cheat!"

"Good luck getting her to believe you on that point." Silvio waved his hand at Stephanie. "How does it feel to be rejected and alone because of what you believe, God-girl?"

Stephanie gathered up her things and looked at her four former group members. "I wish I could say it has never happened before."

Thanksgiving Day
John 6:25-35

Hungering and Thirsting for More

Simon hung up his coat and came into the kitchen. He took a deep breath and grinned. "Wow that smells incredible! I can't believe you cooked a full thanksgiving dinner!"

Charles stirred some more butter into the mashed potatoes. "Hey, sometimes we need to step up and help out."

"Is Tina still at the airport picking up her folks?" Simon opened the oven to get a glimpse of the turkey.

"Yeah. We flipped a coin to see who would cook dinner." Charles placed the potatoes on the warming tray.

"You lost?"

"You know how crazy it is at the airport this week? I won." Charles grinned and looked at the door. "Where's Darla and the kids?"

"Playing with your dog in the backyard. You know how they both love that mutt." Simon shook his head. "Anything I can do?"

Charles looked around the kitchen. "Not right now. How about some coffee?"

Simon grabbed a mug and sat as Charles poured some for himself and then his friend. "So before everyone else gets here, how's it going?"

"Honestly? Not great." Charles sighed. "We're trying to keep a brave face for the kids but things are rough."

Simon nodded. "I hear you. The news keeps on about how things are getting better but I sure don't see it at work.

They keep talking about cut backs and there are always rumors of layoffs."

"Yeah, work is a stress that's for sure." Charles played with the handle on his mug.

Simon watched his friend for a few moments before taking a drink from his mug. "You and Tina still fighting?"

"Nothing ever seems to be good enough for her." Charles sighed. "Although honestly I know I'm a big part of the problem. Have you ever felt that there is something more, something greater in life than simply living from week to week and from crisis to crisis?"

Simon nodded. "I have."

"I wish I knew what it was." Charles eyed his friend. "What?"

"You need Jesus in your life."

"Huh?" Charles took his hand off his mug. "I grew up in the church. I was baptized the same Sunday you were."

"Uh-huh and when was the last time you were in church?"

Charles looked over at the calendar. "I guess it has been a while. Life is busy."

"Yeah it is. Too busy to ignore the most important part." Simon sipped at his coffee. "I've always been straight with you and I'm telling you to get back to church. You need Jesus."

Charles looked at his friend. "I don't know whether Tina will go with me or not. She never was a big church goer."

"Ask her. You might be surprised."

Charles leaned forward. "You know something I don't know?"

Simon shrugged. "All I know is what you are telling me. You say both of you are unhappy because it seems like there is something missing. You say that both of you are having trouble with the stress of trying to raise kids and make a living. Go to church and reconnect with the only one who can help your life and give it meaning."

Charles frowned. "You have the same problems I have in life. You just said your job is stressful and uncertain. Your life is no better than mine."

"Hey, I'm just telling you what I know." Simon downed the last of his coffee. "I know that without Jesus I would be never satisfied and I would be falling apart."

"So you admit that your life isn't perfect?"

"Absolutely." Simon pushed his mug to the center of the table. "But I know that whatever happens I don't have to face it alone. I have the grace and love of God to show me the way and the bread of life and living water to give me strength."

Charles stroked his chin in thought. The sound of a car door slamming and people greeting each other sounded from the yard.

Simon looked out the window. "I think everyone is here. Anything I can do to help?"

"Sure you can help me serve." Charles pushed his chair in and turned to face his friend. "And if in the rush of family and food today if I forget let me just say this — I'm thankful you're here and talked to me."

Simon tilted his head to one side. "So you'll think about going back to church?"

"I'll do you one better. How about we sit together this Sunday?" Charles opened up his arms.

Simon grinned from ear to ear as he embraced his friend.

Other Titles by Peter Andrew Smith

AllThings Are Ready
Communion Prayers for the
Church Year and Pastoral Occasions
10-digit ISBN: 0-7880-2487-6
13-digit ISBN: 978-0-7880-2487-0
$11.95; ebook $8.95

Contributor to
Lectionary Stories for Preaching and Teaching, Cycle A
10-digit ISBN: 0-7880-2704-2
13-digit ISBN: 978-0-7880-2704-8
$19.95; ebook $9.95

Contributor to
Lectionary Tales for the Pulpit, Series VII, Cycle B
10-digit ISBN: 0-7880-2665-8
13-digit ISBN: 978-0-7880-2665-2
$19.95; ebook $9.95

www.ingramcontent.com/pod-product-compliance
Lightning Source LLC
Chambersburg PA
CBHW061300110426
42742CB00012BA/1996